# DARKNESS
# EXPOSED
*Passages from the Spirit*

*Barb Engels*

*Barbara Engels*

# Dedication

———⊕⊕⊕———

To my Lord and Savior Jesus Christ, who gave me the words to write, thank you.

To my husband Fred, thank you for your love and support.

To my sons, Fred Jr. and Stephen, thank you for your patience and love while writing this manuscript.

# Acknowledgements

———⚬⚬⚬———

Claudette Steier, my dear friend, you helped me see I had the words to write. Thank you, Claudette.

To my mom, Eleanor Shuttleworth, thank you for leading me to the foot of the cross, where I met our Lord and Savior, Jesus Christ. Thank you for your prayers and support. I love you.

At the time of this third printing, my mom is now in glory. I miss you mom!

To my brothers and sisters in Christ who have prayed and supported me through the completion of this manuscript. You were there with me through each passage. Praise the Lord!

Thank you Cori, for the hours you spent editing the first printing of this book. I praise and thank God that He chose you. Through Christ, we did it.

DARKNESS EXPOSED


PASSAGES FROM THE SPIRIT

———∞∞∞———

C ome, take a walk through the pages of this book. Can you identify with any of these agonizing souls? Come and see if there is an answer to the questions bombarding you daily.

The people who walked in darkness
Have seen a great light;
Those who dwelt in the land of the
shadow of death,
Upon them a light has shined.

Isaiah 9:2

# Foreword

⸻ ❦ ⸻

I stood still, looking down into a gaping hole, shuddering inside. How did I get here? Where was I? This blackness was not like the darkness of the night. I couldn't see my hand in front of my face.

Wait a minute! Just moments ago I was standing on the edge, and now I am right in the middle of this darkness.

Walking along, fear grips me. Fear captivates me. I am afraid of everything. I am afraid of me. Fear is all around, laughing at me and prodding me on. I drink a substance. It seems to help me forget for a time that I am afraid. The chaos and turmoil swirled around me, suffocating me. I felt alone. No one understood the emptiness I was experiencing inside.

\* \* \* \* \*

Was this darkness growing darker? I tried running away but found I couldn't get away. Yes, this was it. I would end it all. Though fear always had the upper hand, this time I knew I could do it.

*****

Darkness covers the land. Each heart weighs heavily, burdened with the cares and worries of the day. Fear controls our racing hearts, causing many to slip off into eternity without hope.

Our eyes peer hesitantly into this darkness. We take each step cautiously, not knowing which way to go. Our dreams turn rancid. Where is that well—lit pathway we once knew as children?

Disease and sickness run rampant. With no means to ease the pain, many die from their maladies.

Hatred consumes our souls. Growing atrocities mar our hearts as the tentacles of darkness reach out across the globe. 'Self' rules supreme. We step on our neighbor to appease 'self'. Where 'self' rules, there is no room for anyone else.

We toil long into the night, the dollar looming ever before us our only reward. We so love the almighty dollar that we give our souls in exchange for money. Yet the dollars quickly slip away and the cycle begins once again.

Looking down the dusty corridors of our lives, opening many doors along the way, we find only despair and death. Yet we are still hopeful of finding the door that leads to peace. Many are the well—beaten paths that lead to emptiness. We follow after evil, and evil fills our hearts. Evil's death grip suffocates as it holds us in its clutches. Weariness takes its toll, and the pressures of life weigh us down.

Where was I? The realization came to me. I was looking into my own soul.

# A Guide to the Passages

---

### Passage One

I just meant to take one little look at that fabulous—looking girl across the hall. I didn't mean to flirt with her. After all, I'm married and in love with the woman I married. Now here I am sleeping next to someone I don't even know. How did this happen?

\*\*\*\*\*

### Passage Two

Witnessing Christ: A woman caught in adultery.

\*\*\*\*\*

### Passage Three

How can I live with myself? I am plagued with this horrible disease. I know I will die. I never thought this would happen to me. Life is so unfair.

*****

### Passage Four

I'm only a child. I'm all alone in a war-torn world. Mama, I need you, please don't leave me alone!

*****

### Passage Five

Witnessing Christ: The bread and the fishes.

*****

### Passage Six

How could a few drinks hurt? I clutched the degree tightly in my fist, remembering how hard I had worked for it. This celebration was just what I needed to ease the strain of four years.

*****

### Passage Seven

My body ached. It didn't matter which way I turned. Every muscle screamed with pain. I awoke in a pool of blood.

\*\*\*\*\*

### Passage Eight

You were once enlightened to the truth, you knew the Way.

\*\*\*\*\*

### Passage Nine

As the fine white powder, drifted up into my nostrils, an explosion of colors and absolute power filled my body. I could live forever.

\*\*\*\*\*

### Passage Ten

Witnessing Christ: Peace be still.

\*\*\*\*\*

### Passage Eleven

I loved her but hated her at the same time. I tried to figure out what I as doing wrong. Maybe if I loved her more, she wouldn't hit me, she wouldn't hurt me anymore.

*****

### Passage Twelve

What else could I do? I had to get even. Life was so unfair. I had the perfect plan. She cheated on me, and would have to pay. I had watched enough through life to know I could get away with it. No one would ever find out.

*****

### Passage Thirteen

Witnessing Christ: The miracle of the withered hand.

*****

### Passage Fourteen

I was thankful for being on my own, but fearful of the days ahead. Being on the streets kept me in constant danger.

\*\*\*\*\*

### Passage Fifteen

I'm my own person. I don't need anyone to look after me. Why was I shut away in this institution? I want out!

\*\*\*\*\*

### Passage Sixteen

Witnessing     Christ:     Death     is raised to life.

\*\*\*\*\*

### Passage Seventeen

Bitterness and hatred consumed me, leaving a foulness that I can actually taste. How did I get like this?

\*\*\*\*\*

*Passage Eighteen*

## Witnessing Christ: Crucify Him!

# Passage One

———⊷∞⊶———

S lamming the door with so much force, I thought I'd felt the foundations shake. I didn't know what I was going to do! Angry tears spilled down my face.

Why did he have to tell me that he had been with another woman? And yet, it was as if I wanted, even needed, to hear all the details. But no details were to be had. He suddenly kept silent, and in my imagination I saw the act-taking place before my eyes. What had I ever done to deserve this kind of treatment?

My heart felt crushed, broken into a million pieces. The weight of his words made my stomach churn until I thought I would be literally sick.

As I pounded the table with my fists, rage and bitterness began to take over. "Well, this is it! I'll never forgive him. He can rot in hell!"

I didn't care that he said it had been a mistake. What right did he have to try and make things better? He broke his vows and now he would have to pay!

I began to imagine things I could do to make his life miserable. He wouldn't get away with this!

An empty loneliness crept over me as I stared out the window, looking for a way out, not knowing which way to turn.

I began to think about my life. What would I do now? Everyone would know. What would people think?

Was I to blame? Maybe it was me, and it was some-how my fault? "No," I shouted, "I didn't break my vows!"

In the recesses of my mind, something I had heard a long time ago came back to me: "Jesus loves me this I know, for the Bible tells me so." I tried to ignore it. I didn't feel loved. The only one I believed cared for me had just rejected me. But this persistent thought kept infiltrating my thought patterns.

"I love you," a voice called out.

Was I losing my mind? Where was this voice coming from? It filled my kitchen, filled my thoughts, vibrating throughout my surroundings.

"I love you," the voice repeated. "I know what you are feeling. Man rejected Me; I was hated and spat upon. A man close to Me sold Me for a few pieces of silver. My best friend denied Me. Yes, I understand. You can be made whole, and love will come to you once again. Allow Me to set you free. I so deeply love you, that if you were the only person in the world, I would still have gone to the cross and died for you. My blood was spilled on the cross so you could walk in My freedom."

What was happening to me? Just hearing His voice and the love instilled in each word caused me to let go of all the hurt, rejection, hatred, anger, frustration, and loneliness.

"Why would You do this for me?" I cried.

"It's very simple," He replied. "I love you."

"Cast all of your care, all of your disappointments, all of your anxious thoughts, and lay them here at My feet. Let Me carry this load for you. And if you could find it in your heart to forgive, then no bitterness or sorrow of heart can tie you into knots. I will help you walk through these emotions. In Me there is perfect rest."

I was totally over-whelmed. Yes, I needed a release from the fears, the torments, the ugly thoughts, the hatred I had for this other woman, and the bitterness I felt towards my husband. I craved this freedom being offered to me.

I called out to Him. "Jesus, I accept what You are offering. Please come into my heart and make me whole. Give me the freedom to love again. I surrender all."

I sat for the longest time, pondering these things in my heart. I wondered how I would act when my husband came through the door that evening.

Later, I heard the car pull into the garage. In that instant I felt butterflies. I hadn't felt that for him in such a very long time. Jesus Christ was true to His promise. New love sprang up in me for him, this man I had married.

I met my husband at the door and melted into his arms. As I looked up at him, tears glistened in his eyes.

We would walk through this life hand in hand. We would not take each other for granted. We would work on loving each other and learning how to forgive.

# *Passage Two*

— ∞∞ —

With every opportunity that presented itself, I wanted to be near this man they called Jesus.

Many people from different tribes and cultures had joined together that early morning on the entrance steps leading to the temple. Some were there because of the interesting things they had heard about this man, others out of curiosity, still others to get a glimpse of this new teacher. I was there because the more I heard Him speak, the more I wanted to hear Him.

As He began to talk, a great commotion could be heard taking place on a street adjacent to us. We all arose to our feet to see what was happening. I couldn't believe my eyes, when a procession of angry men descended upon us! They were half carrying, half dragging a nearly naked woman, and pushing her towards Jesus.

Terror was etched on the woman's face.

What had she done to deserve such treatment? I'm sure that was the question on everyone's mind at that precise moment. Someone near to her handed her their cloak, and she quickly wrapped it around herself.

It was then I recognized the men to be those of the temple itself, the Scribes and Pharisees. I shivered inside. What had happened to these people that they should be so possessed with hatred?

One of the men shouted angrily at Jesus. "This woman was found right in the act of committing adultery!"

Another man, in the next breath, shouted accusingly, "In the law, Moses declares we are to stone such a one! What do you say, Jesus?"

With everything happening before us, not one person had even noticed what Jesus was doing through all of this. As we looked over to Him, He was on one knee, looking down, and drawing a stick over the hard-packed ground. I found this hard to understand. At any moment, I expected Him to deal harshly with the men just as they had dealt with the woman. But Jesus kept silent and did not even look up. This seemed to aggravate the men even more.

One man stepped closer to Jesus demandingly and shouted louder. Maybe he thought Jesus hadn't heard the first time, although everyone in the square was now glued to the scene in front of them. "Well, Jesus, what do you say we should do?" he demanded roughly.

It was then Jesus lifted His eyes, and spoke to the men who surrounded Him and the woman.

"You without sin, toss the first stone."

Each word He spoke was filled with such conviction; I checked my own heart to see if sin was lingering there.

The crowd of angry men began to disperse. Each one hung their heads, as they crept away in the early morning light. Soon not one of the men remained.

Jesus stood up and looked around. He then spoke with such love to the woman, as He asked, "Where are your accusers?"

The woman answered with a hesitant voice, "There—is no one here—to accuse me, Lord."

"Well, neither do I accuse you. Go and sin no more."

I watched as the woman's face seemed to transform before my eyes. She began to glow. The fear had melted away and in it's place, a love and confidence shone forth. She lifted her head, smiled, and walked away with new assurance filling each step. Her self-respect had returned. She no longer needed to hide. She was forgiven. Jesus had given her a reason to live.

I pondered over what had just taken place. This man, Jesus, wasn't like any man I had ever known, and yet did I really know Him? Everything I thought I had known before was irrelevant. I just wanted to know everything about Jesus. Some people were saying He was just a good teacher, but He was more. I could hear it in His voice; I could see it in His eyes. He was more than a mere teacher, more than a man. Was He God, manifest in the flesh?

I had given up everything and everybody to follow this man Jesus. No one had understood my decision, but an unexplainable force drew me.

I noticed that Jesus seemed ready to move on. I almost felt His mission this morning was accomplished, and it was time for Him to go on to His next assignment.

I didn't feel a special calling like some of the men seemed to, but I didn't care. I just wanted to be with Him. Though I followed from a distance, Jesus didn't once ask me to leave. He would look at me once in a while as He spoke to the crowds, and smile knowingly. That glance would cause a deep burning inside of me, and I knew I would follow Him wherever His journey would take Him.

*****

I sat at my desk, my heart pounding. Had I really been back in Bible times? Or had I just been sleeping? Something had definitely taken place and I was not sure what. But one thing I knew for certain, I wanted to know more about Jesus. Journeying though the pages of the Bible, I planned to explore every word that set forth.

# Passage Three

---

A IDS! I heard the doctor speak these words to me, but he couldn't really have meant me. This kind of thing happened to other people, but not to me.

Didn't he know that AIDS was a death sentence? Did anyone ever recover from this dreaded disease? I would be an outcast, a leper.

The doctor was speaking to me, but I seemed unable to comprehend what he was saying. He said something about being in the full-blown stage, and that I had but six months to live. He must be kidding. That's it, he's mixed up his records, and he's got the wrong person. Sure, I had been a little run down lately, and peculiar sores were appearing all over my body, but this couldn't be AIDS! Having this heavy laid on me was more than I could take.

I began to think back on what my mother had said when I told her of my decision to live with a male friend. She said, "God made us male and female," and that what I was doing was going totally against God. She also said that what I sowed, I would one day reap. I remembered the sadness in her eyes when I left. She hugged me and said she would be praying for me. I told her not to pray. I didn't need God and I didn't need her prayers. Silent tears ran down her cheeks, and I told myself she would get over it. But now as I sat there in the doctor's office, her words started to ring true, and there was no escaping the reality of my situation. How would I be able to tell her? I still didn't want to believe it myself.

I don't really remember what else the doctor said. Everything was a blur. He put his hand on my shoulder, though, saying he'd see me next week, and prescribed a drug to ease the pain.

I had long since moved out from my friend's apartment, and was now living on my own. But what had taken place in those two years I had lived with him had sealed my fate. The doctor had said he would contact him, and have him come in for a checkup. I now regretted having ever known him.

Six months to live! I was shaken to the core of my being. I was so young (only twenty-five), had a very good job, and now I was going to die. Was this fair? Anger rose up inside of me. I would fight this thing. Death could not have me. But where was this coming from? I had always been a coward. A little cold had me sniveling and seeking attention. What would I do with a thing like AIDS? The doctor had said something about pain. I wouldn't be able to bear pain!

I finally arrived home to my cozy apartment, and collapsed on the bed. I began to sob uncontrollably, my body heaving with the weight of the doctor's words.

I had not been in contact with my family for nearly three years. I was more than ashamed to call them now, but I had a yearning to see my mother again. My dad had said I repulsed him, so I knew I wouldn't get any sympathy from him. Yet it wasn't sympathy I was seeking. I was afraid to die. What I really needed was the reassurance that what Mother had said to me, all through those earlier years while I was growing up, was true. I needed to find out once and for all. I felt a little hope spring up in me, but also a fear that she wouldn't want anything to do with me once she knew the truth.

I called that evening and was thankful that Mother had answered the phone. I explained to her that I needed to see her. Would she come? She said she would be on the next plane and that dad would accompany her. I wanted to scream no! I just wanted her, but fearing that she wouldn't come at all, I held my tongue.

My mother and dad sat on the sofa across from me. It was great to see them again. They commented that I looked a little pale. I began to feel fearful, and wondered how I would explain the predicament I found myself in. Dad kept looking around the apartment, expecting at any moment to be confronted with the other man. I decided to put him at ease. I explained to them both that I was no longer living in a relationship with another man. I paused then, my heart racing within me. But because of this relationship, I had contracted AIDS.

You could have heard a pin drop. Dad rose to his feet, came over, and knelt beside me. He put his arms around me and began to weep, quietly at first, but then loud sobs erupted from his soul. I wept with him. Mother quietly joined us. After some time, Mother and Dad pulled themselves together. It was Dad who spoke first.

"Son," he said quietly, "before anything else is said, Mother and I strongly believe that Jesus Christ will forgive you of your past, and that if you believe and ask Him into your heart, you will live eternally with Him." Dad took a deep breath at this point and continued. "Just two years ago, when you left . . . I could hardly bear the thought of you living with another man . . . I blamed myself for your behavior."

I wanted to protest, but Dad asked me to wait until he finished saying what he felt had to be said.

"I always pushed your mother aside with all of her religious talk, but the words she had spoken to me would never leave. Those words haunted me! They followed me wherever I went. There was no getting away from the love, either." Dad then smiled at Mother and squeezed her hand in his. Tears threatened to spill over once again, but Dad held them in check.

"It was late one night, and I had stopped in the bar for a few beers before coming home. Mother had said that very morning, the only way we were going to get our son back was to pray, to agree together, and take authority over the evil one who was out to destroy our son. Those words triggered something in me when two men strolled into the bar, arm in arm. Such anger rose up in me. I knew then what needed to be done. At this point, I didn't even know Jesus Christ, but I was eager to get home and pray with your mother. So your mother led me in the sinner's prayer. Together we pray for you everyday, doing warfare on your behalf. I believe our prayers have been answered."

I bowed my head and began to weep. I was overwhelmed with what I had just heard. Dad had been a very hard man, and what I saw in him now was a love I had never known.

"Yes," I cried, "I want this love to fill my soul!"

My parents that evening led me to Jesus Christ.

Mother and Dad offered to take me home with them, to nurse me during the final stages AIDS would take me through. I agreed, as I didn't want to die alone. But the thought of being alone didn't bother me as much anymore because I now knew Jesus, and somewhere inside, I sensed He would look after me, no matter what the days ahead had in store.

One of the first physical organs to be taken from me were my eyes. Not only couldn't I see, but also this gruesome virus attacked every fiber of my being. I had no appetite. I became like a skeleton with skin stretched over it. Large open sores covered my body and seeped daily. I felt sorry for the nurse who attended these craters.

But this was no ordinary run-of-the-mill nurse, who Mother and Dad had hired to look after all of my needs. There was something special in her touch. The best I could possibly explain it was, her hands felt like how Jesus would touch me. Another interesting thing was that she would pray for me in a language I didn't understand. I asked her about it one day, and she explained that with this language she knew she was praying the Will of God for my life. I began noticing, after she prayed for me like this, a new strength filling me. I almost felt like I wasn't going to die. But to look at me, all the factors pointed to death. I had never heard of anybody being snatched from the claws of AIDS. It was indeed a killer.

The nurse read daily to me from God's Holy Word. I was over-whelmed. Yes, I needed miracles Jesus performed. People who had leprosy were healed! Hope began to spring up in me like new grass springing up after a long, hard winter. I began questioning. Would Jesus heal me? Was that same power available today? Jesus says in His Word, He is the same yesterday, today and tomorrow.

I remembered how Jesus healed the blind man. The blind man was sitting at the edge of the road. He heard the throngs of people, the exciting details on everyone's lips of how Jesus was passing by, and that He was passing by today! The blind man called out to Jesus, "Son of David, have mercy on me!" He could sense the crowd stopping, and knew that Jesus had turned around to face him. Jesus called the man forward.

"What is it you would have Me do for you?"

"Oh, Jesus, that I may see!"

Jesus spoke to him again, "Go your way, your faith has made you whole."

Immediately the man's sight was restored.

I remember how faith began to grow in me as I heard these words spoken. As I listened intently to the Words from this Holy Book, truly began to receive strength.

I was now well into the fifth month of this debilitating disease since being diagnosed. I knew my body was wasting away, though I couldn't see what was happening. Then I asked Mother and Dad to agree with me in prayer for my total healing. They agreed eagerly. Knowing that if God could bring me to my knees, then God could heal me. Sometimes I was discouraged, but when those days were too much for me to bear the nurse would put on beautiful worship music, and I felt my spirit soaring on angels' wings.

I don't know the day, but as I was sleeping, Jesus appeared to me. The beauty of His Presence took my breath away. He took me by the hand and said He wanted to show me something. I went eagerly with Him. We came to an open square. Soldiers marched forward, leading a man stripped to the waist, and tied him to a pole. The man didn't protest or try to escape. He just submitted to their treatment. I felt I needed to help, but I couldn't move. I glanced around but Jesus was nowhere to be seen. I was transfixed as the scene unfolded before me. A Roman soldier was whipping the man tied to the pole. The whip had metal on the end of it, and with each lash, the flesh on the man's back tore open. Blood splattered everywhere, and I could see deep furrows in the man's flesh. Bone was visible. The man did not cry out. I was sick of this sight, and began to weep freely. What had this man done? I tried to come to his aid but was helpless. When they untied him, the man rose slowly to his feet and turned to face me. It was Jesus!

"With these stripes, you are healed!" Jesus proclaimed triumphantly. "You are to share this miracle with the ones I will bring you to. I have called you to be My voice to a sick and dying world."

Incredible warmth covered me. I felt like someone was pouring warm water over me. It seemed as if I was being cradled in strong arms of love.

The first thing I did was open my eyes. I could see! Sunlight was streaming in through a window to my left. I began to feel stronger and stronger, so I put my legs over the side of the bed, and slowly sat up. I was thrilled! I had only been able to lift my head, and now my entire body was sitting up. I wondered if I was trying to do too much, but the excitement flowing through me spurred me on. Where the sores had been was now new flesh. There wasn't a single sore to be found on my body. I felt like a new man. I was a new man. I raised my arms and began to thank and praise Jesus for healing me. There were no words to describe my joy, and to my further delight, my heavenly Father gave me a new language in which to praise Him. My cries of joy filled the house.

I heard footsteps coming quickly down the hall, and my door flew open. Mother and Dad stood in the open doorway, and the sight of me held them in awe!

"Oh, son," they cried together, "Jesus is true to His Word, you are healed!"

We cried and jumped up and down together for joy. All this exertion took my breath away, but it truly felt wonderful to be alive.

The next person to share in my healing was my faithful nurse. She was ecstatic! I knew Jesus had brought her to me, and we would share in this ministry together.

\*\*\*\*\*

We opened a Hospice Centre for AIDS patients, sharing with them my miracle, and also the miracle of being reborn in Jesus Christ. Some never see a physical healing, but all have the hope of living with Jesus eternally.

# Passage Four

———⊗⊗⊗———

Earsplitting explosions jerked my eyes open. What I thought had been a dream was actually a horrible reality. I heard loud screams escaping from my mouth, but it didn't sound like my voice at all. It felt like I was in a hole, a dark hole! My eyes, now grown accustomed to the blackness, confirmed this impression. I was in a hole! How did I get here? Where were Mama and Papa? Where was my little brother? Then my mind was pierced with the horror of what had happened.

I could see the terror on Papa's face as strangers burst into our house, and began firing their weapons on us as we sat eating our evening meal. We were helpless! Bullets ripped apart everything in their path, including my parents. I remember ducking under the kitchen table. Then the whole house exploded and debris went flying everywhere. What happened after that, however, was a total mystery.

I needed to find my bearings. Where was I? I inched my way along what seemed to be a long tunnel. The stench burned my eyes, and bile rose up in my throat. After some time, I came to an entrance with an iron ladder leading upwards. I began my ascent, my body stiff, my legs not wanting to move. At the top there was a casing over the hole. After much effort I finally was able to move it aside. Fresh air assaulted my nostrils, and I gulped it with thankfulness. My legs wobbled as I stood to my feet. I slowly looked around. As far as the eye could see was total destruction. Where a building once stood, now was rubble. Smoke was rising into the early morning light along the horizon. Suddenly I was overcome by grief, grief for my parents, my little brother and now my city. Everything was gone! I was all alone. How would I survive? Out of the corner of my eye, I saw a figure dart into the rubble. I quickly ran over to the spot. Someone else was alive! But he wasn't as happy to see me, as I was to see him. He looked to be about my age, eleven — maybe twelve. He was poorly dressed. His face, smudged with dirt, snarled back at me.

"Look, kid, I'm not sharing this with anyone, so get lost!" He turned to leave with his newfound treasure.

"I don't want anything from you," I protested, "I just want to know who you are and what's happening."

He looked back at me in disbelief. "What do you mean, what's happening? Where have you been? By the looks of you, you must be one of those rich kids." He came toward me in a threatening way. I edged backwards. He smiled, knowing he had the upper hand, but didn't take any more steps toward me. His eyes narrowed thoughtfully, as if a plan was forming in his mind. "Look," he said, "we need each other. It's better to have two looking for food. What do you say?"

I nodded shyly. What did I have to lose? My whole world was gone.

He explained to me, as we went scrounging for food, that our country was at war. No one could be trusted. The people in power were fighting amongst themselves. Their desire for power and their greed had plunged our country into chaos. Both sides wanted to win, but instead, innocent people died everywhere to gain this so-called freedom. His bitter words filled me with fear. My papa worked with the government! This hatred for the government had taken the lives of my family. Tears came to my eyes, but not wanting him to see, I turned my back and went about my business of looking through the rubble for something substantial to call my own.

Several months passed, but the day to day struggle was life threatening. You had to be on the lookout for soldiers who fired on any moving object, whether predators looking for food, or your supposed friends. Living in the sewers during winter was a blessing in disguise, for at least there was warmth from all the other bodies, but the putrid smell caused us to seek fresh air above ground at regular intervals.

I wandered over to our old neighborhood one day, to see where I once lived. The memory of that horror-filled day assaulted me. I re-lived the nightmare of it constantly. I decided to face my fears head on. Our stately house was a pile of rubble. Tremors of hopelessness ran through me. Somewhere under this rubble lay the bodies of my beloved parents and my little brother. I still did not know how I survived. I let the pent-up anger and grief take over. I don't know how long I stood there, tears flowing down my cheeks. I then felt a hand on my shoulder. I wheeled around, and a man stood facing me. I panicked! Right away I noticed he wasn't carrying a gun, but that didn't mean he wasn't dangerous. He spoke to me in a language I didn't understand, but in such a peaceful way, a caring way. I decided to stay put. He was beckoning me to come with him. He saw the hesitation, the distrust in my eyes, for then he came closer and offered me his hand. All odds were against me. If he were to kill me, I didn't stand a chance, for I was in his grip. But his hand felt comforting, like that of my mother. New tears threatened to spill over. I ached to be held by Mama again.

The stranger took me to a makeshift building, which held hundreds of people, from babies to kids my age, up to adults. The man took me over to one of the long tables and signaled me to wait. I sat there, glancing around the building. It was amazing to see everyone so happy. A tug on my arm brought me back from my thoughts, and fresh emotions burst forth. There stood my little brother! He wasn't dead! We grabbed one another and hugged each other. Our tears mingled as we kissed each other's cheeks. I didn't know God, but I thanked Him all the same, for bringing a loved one back to me.

My brother explained that Samaritan's Purse was an organization from North America. They were in the process of building an orphanage. Missionaries were going to come and look after as many children as they could. He went on to say that we were on the list, and we now had a home.

That evening we were given a feast. After eating on the streets, hot soup and bread was a feast. When we had finished our meal, the stranger who brought me here, spoke (through one of our own people) words, which filled me with hope. He said that a man named Jesus Christ knew what we were going through. He made a Way for us to live eternally with Him in a place where there wasn't any war, bloodshed, or greed, but only love, joy, and peace. He went on to say that Jesus Christ shed His blood and died for our sins, so that if we believed in Him, we could have eternal life.

From what I could see, without Jesus Christ, there wasn't any hope. With my limited understanding, I stood to my feet and walked to the front of the room where the stranger was standing. I explained to the man speaking for the stranger that I wanted to know this man, Jesus. His eyes lit up and then he spoke to the stranger. The stranger knelt down beside me and bowed his head. A movement caused me to look around. There stood my brother. He too, knelt with us. As the stranger prayed, incredible warmth and happiness filled my heart. I now had a new friend.

My surroundings had not changed. I was still living in a war zone. But I knew that whatever happened, I would take Jesus Christ with me wherever I went. I would take Jesus into the sewers to share this new life with others living underground. My childhood was brutally ripped away from me. My responsibility was now to take care of my brother, but with Jesus Christ in my heart, I could accomplish anything.

# Passage Five

—⚬⚬⚬—

I stood trembling on a grassy mountain-side. What I had just witnessed was truly a miraculous event. Five thousand people, men, women, and children had followed Jesus to this deserted mountainside, late in the day and far past the dinner hour. I overheard Jesus speaking to one of his disciples.

"At this hour, where can we buy bread, so these people may eat?" Jesus questioned his disciple.

The disciple looked somewhat bewildered. "Master, it would take at least two hundred denarii to feed this crowd, and then they would not have enough to satisfy their hunger."

Jesus stood back, allowing His disciple to think this problem through. It seemed impossible! I couldn't imagine, without substantial means, providing for even ten people. Was Jesus expecting His disciples to feed over five thousand men, plus their families?

It didn't take long before one of the other disciples stepped forward, a small boy at his side. "Jesus, there is a small lad here with five barley loaves and two small fish, but I can't see how these could feed so many."

Jesus smiled at the boy. He then asked His disciples to arrange the people in groups of fifty. This in itself was no small task. After it was accomplished, Jesus took the barley loaves and lifted His eyes toward heaven and gave thanks. He broke the loaves in pieces and gave them to the disciples to distribute. He followed the same procedure with the fish.

I watched closely. Each company of fifty ate and were satisfied. The bread and the fish multiplied before my very eyes. How could this be?

Jesus spoke again to his disciples. "Gather up the remaining fragments, so that nothing is lost."

The disciples went about gathering up the remaining food, and twelve baskets full were recovered.

It began to dawn on me then, we truly possessed the means to feed a starving world. The heartrending photos publishers displayed in their magazines constantly tugged my heart. But, I would rationalize, what could one person do for so many dying of starvation? Jesus had just given me the answer. The small lad had come forward to share his meager lunch, and Jesus miraculously multiplied the bread and the fish. Jesus often said he was the same yesterday, today, and tomorrow. What He did yesterday, I believed He would do today. I could hardly wait to put this theory of giving into practice.

# Passage Six

———— ∞∞∞ ————

Trapped! Panic seized me. What was happening? I could hear the sound of scurrying feet around me, and excited whispers, but I could do nothing to respond. Blackness enveloped me. I felt like I was drowning, unable to breathe. Then the sensation of drowning ceased and air rushed into my lungs.

All was deathly quiet. The whispers had stopped. I wondered if this maybe was death. But didn't I once hear that heaven was full of light?

Heaven. What right did I have to think about heaven? I scoffed at my sister, calling her a religious nut, a fanatic, a holy roller. No, I didn't deserve heaven. Anyway, I had too much living to do to worry about the afterlife. I had the world by the tail. I just finished university and would be walking into my Father's business as vice president. We owned a million dollar company, and I vowed after getting my education, I would extend the existing capital into billions. Just thinking about this made me eager to get started on my new career.

What puzzled me at the moment was why I couldn't move? Why wouldn't my eyelids open? Where was I? I felt cased in cement. I didn't want to feel like this. I used to be in control. What was happening? I heard whispers again, and strained to hear what was being said.

Wait a minute! I recognized that voice. It seemed so far away, but I caught the words, "I love you, I'm praying for you, you can make it, hang in there, and don't leave us." It was definitely my sister. Why would I be going anywhere? I had too much to do. My brain felt numb, but I tried to remember what happened. Yes, I was at a celebration some of the guys at the school were holding in my honor. My Dad, for a graduation present, gave me a Porsche. It was my dream car. My dad wasn't the kind of guy to just hand you something, you had to earn it. I worked hard for that car and for the successful career that was soon to be mine. But something was very wrong. My recollection of the previous evening was just out of reach, and the harder I thought about it, the further away it seemed.

Voices were once again penetrating the fog in my mind. Why was it impossible to respond? My sister was speaking again, her voice now clearer and louder. "Dad is right here beside you. Please if you can hear us, open your eyes!"

"Son, I'm right here—" Dad's voice broke and I could hear him sobbing.

I had never heard my dad cry before. It sounded foreign to me. My eyelids felt heavy and cumbersome, but I tried willing them to open. There was no response. I then began to bargain with God who I didn't know. "Look, if you are really out there, please let me open my eyes. Just this one little thing, and next time I'm in church I'll throw a few bucks into the plate." I had an inheritance coming to me from my grandfather when I turned twenty-one, so I imagined I could spare a few bucks. The rare times when I had darkened the door of a church, that's all

I heard coming from the pulpit, their need of finances. Weren't they always in dire need of funds? Still no response. So, God couldn't be bought off.

My sister's voice could be heard once again. "It's okay, you can try again tomorrow. Don't give up, you are on every prayer chain in town. I'll be back tomorrow." And with that all was silent.

One thing was certain, I wasn't at home. I reached back into my memory for pieces that would explain the dilemma I found myself in. Something was tugging at my memory. Yes, I was at a party. Then I was sitting in my new car with my best friend. We had decided to take a cruise to see what the car could do. I'd only had a few drinks and was well in control. The speed of the car exhilarated us both. What I remember next were headlights bearing down on us, and swerving to miss the inevitable. I could hear myself screaming, but no sound came out.

"Heavenly Father, as You already know, my brother is lying in this hospital bed unable to move. He doesn't know You. But I know Your mercy reaches into places we can't comprehend. I ask You to prepare the way for him to come to know You. We don't deserve Your love and kindness to us, Father, but it belongs to us because of Jesus Christ, for He paid our way back to You. Please bring this circumstance around for good, Father. I trust You will work all things out in Your time."

My sister's prayer jarred me back. I was beginning to understand the seriousness of my condition. What was so horrifying through all of this was that I couldn't respond, even though all that was within me desperately wanted to reach out and make contact with my loved ones. For the life of me, though, I couldn't understand why my sister found it so important to be in contact with a God she couldn't see. Besides, I wasn't a bad person. I partied a little, but went to church at Christmas and gave to well-meaning causes. Why was my sister so intent on preaching to us about needing a Savior? But as I began to reflect on this, I had to admit I needed someone's help at this point in my life. For now, I couldn't do anything for myself.

Angry voices broke the silence in my room. "He killed my son and now he has to pay! I don't care how much money he has, or his family, for that matter. I want to see some justice done!" cried an angry woman.

The nurse in charge tried to calm the distraught woman. "Look, you barging in here will not help. I believe justice has been served. This young man will never walk again. Even if he does come out of this coma, his chances of a normal life are very slim." The voices faded off into the hallway, but the nurse's words haunted me. What was she saying, never to lead a normal life again? I could hear, that was normal! So my friend had been killed in the accident. I had feared as much, and now it was a reality. Why had I been so foolish to get behind the wheel of the car after consuming those drinks? Maybe I wasn't in control as I had thought. If I was in a coma, how could I hear what was going on? But one fact remained — I could not move. Was this the way I would spend my remaining days, or was I going to die?

I stood near a pool. Surrounding the pool were many sick people: blind, lame, and paralyzed. The rumor was that when there was a moving of the water, if you were the first to step into the pool, you would be healed. Excitement filled me. I was standing! I looked at my body, and it was me all right. What was I doing here? I noticed a man speaking to one of the sick people. I edged closer to hear what was being said. The man intrigued me. I was drawn to Him. He was asking the paralyzed man if he wanted to be made whole. The paralyzed man replied that when he got near the pool, someone always stepped down ahead of him, and they were healed instead. This man then spoke the most powerful words I had ever heard. "Rise, take up your bed and walk!" The next thing I knew, the paralyzed man was healed. He took up his bed and walked.

The man then turned, His eyes looked straight into my soul. I was riveted to the spot where I stood. He spoke similar words to me, "Do you want to be made whole?" I could only nod my head in agreement.

Tears began to stream down my face. "Yes," I cried, "I want to be made well!"

Then He answered, "You are made whole because of your sister's prayers."

Something was happening to me! My eyelids responded and opened. My eyes quickly adjusted to the darkened room. I was in a hospital. I was hooked up to many different machines. I slowly turned my head, and this movement attracted attention from the night nurse. She quickly came to my bedside and spoke into the intercom. "Get the doctor, he's awake."

The doctor bent over me and shone a light into my eyes. He explained there was a tube in my throat and I wouldn't be able to speak, but I was to blink my eyes once for yes and twice for no. He then began to poke and prod, asking me if I could feel anything. Each place he poked me, I blinked once, as I could feel his every touch. Watching the doctor's eyes, I knew this was startling information. He said he would be taking further x-rays tomorrow to confirm whether I was speaking the truth or not. He went on to say that the first x-ray showed my spine severed and my neck was clearly broken. These severe breaks could not be repaired. A body so badly damaged would not walk again. I listened intently to the doctor explain this to me, but I knew that this person, Jesus Christ, who I met in my dream, was a miracle worker, and I wanted to find out more about Him. The doctor and nurses then left, leaving me alone. My eyes scanned the room. I wondered where my sister and dad were. A nurse re-entered the room to say my family had been notified that I had regained consciousness, and they would be right over.

I shut my eyes once again and reflected. If what the doctor had said was indeed a fact, then it was God healing me. This humbled me. I did not know Him. I lived for myself. I was selfish and arrogant. Why would God want to heal me? Was it really because of my sister's prayers? I didn't deserve His favor. I didn't deserve His love. Deep down, I wanted now to have a relationship with this person, Jesus Christ. He was not a sissy's God. He was a God who cared and loved the humans He created. I'm not sure where this knowledge was coming from, but from now on I would be eager to sit and listen, to be educated on who Jesus Christ was and is.

Someone took my hand and I opened my eyes. I was looking into the tearful faces of my dad and my sister. That my dad was not ashamed to cry moved me deeply. This was a miracle in itself. Dad is a proud man. He was well educated, and worked long hours, not letting anyone get in his way as he hurried up the corporate ladder. He is very successful. I wanted to follow in his footsteps, but now I was not so sure this was the route I wanted to take.

My sister was the first to speak. Dad just gripped my hand. "The doctor relayed the good news! You are actually beginning to have feeling? I must admit that when I had people pray for you, I wondered if God would hear our prayers, as you are not a believer. But this just proves God's ways are not our ways. You are going to walk out of here, and all the glory and praise belongs to Jesus Christ."

I was amazed she spoke this way in front of Dad. Dad would never let her speak about her relationship with Jesus.

He used to tell her to keep her religion to herself. What had changed? There were so many questions I wanted to ask my sister, but the doctor had yet to remove the tube from my throat.

Dad spoke next. "Son, you gave us all quite a scare, but now that you are on the mend, we are looking forward to having you home. There are many things I must discuss with you, but they will wait until you are safely home."

Home? Dad had long since removed me from the family home. He had said that my lifestyle wasn't compatible with his, and I should find my own place to live. I opted for living in the dormitory. The inheritance money I would be receiving when I turned twenty-one would not be available for another four months. But when I registered in university, it was four years away. Yet this all seemed so insignificant now. I truly felt I was starting a new life, and what I would do with this money was going to be in the hands of my new friend, Jesus Christ.

My dad and sister said they would let me rest and be back tomorrow. Then they could get a full report from the doctor after he tested me. I smiled and closed my eyes.

Day by day, my body grew stronger and stronger. Many different teams of doctors and nurses paraded into my room daily. Those of the medical profession were astounded, and they themselves were calling it a miracle. The place where my spine had been severed had miraculously fused together. I was soon walking with a cane, and my release from the hospital was imminent. I felt as though they were keeping me detained so doctors from other parts of the country could come and witness this phenomenon. I had no qualms in giving all glory to Jesus Christ. I sat and talked to my sister about my dream where Jesus healed the paralyzed man by the pool. She showed me in the Bible where this had actually taken place. She also told me of a prophetic Word, where young men would dream dreams, and she felt Jesus Christ was calling me into a powerful ministry. I didn't know if this was true or not, but I did hunger and thirst for the realities of Christ.

I had now been home for nearly a month. My dad had also given his life to Christ. He couldn't deny the miracle that had taken place before his eyes. Our relationship has since been healed, and not only do I feel that I have a new life, I also have a new family. With all this excitement, I still felt burdened with guilt, knowing I was responsible for my friend's death. He was dead and I was alive. I remembered the day in the hospital when his mom came into my room. She was very angry and hurt. I began to pray and ask the Lord what I could do to help her. I needed to see her. My dad and sister thought I should just leave it alone, but a gnawing on the inside would not let up. I needed to ask her to forgive me.

My driver's license was suspended for three years, so I asked my sister to take me to my friend's mother. After some coaxing, she finally relented. On the way, I started to feel fearful, wondering if she would see me. But peace began to fill me, and I laid this anxiety before the Lord.

We pulled into her driveway, and before leaving the car, I asked my sister to pray with me. We agreed I would allow the Lord to speak through me, and that in some way my friend's mother also would come to know Jesus Christ as her personal Savior.

She answered the door and asked what we wanted? She didn't recognize me! I hesitated at first, not knowing hot to explain who I was. The words, "I was driving the car the night your son was killed — he was my best friend," stumbled out of my mouth. She stepped back from the doorway and invited us inside. I had no idea what she was thinking by the look on her face.

"I've been praying for you," she began, "though at first I wanted you to die. I was very bitter and angry that my son was killed and you lived. My husband and I were only able to have one child, and now he is gone. Grief has a way of distorting perception. With all the medication I was on, I tried taking my life. But God came to me in my hour of need. My bitterness and anger left, and in their place, love and forgiveness. So I have forgiven you, and I don't hold hatred in my heart for you any longer. No one will ever replace the love I had for my son, but my husband has agreed to adoption, and I'm looking forward to a new child."

I was beside myself with joy and release. We met in the middle of the room and embraced. God is a miraculous God.

# Passage Seven

⸺ ◦∞◦ ⸺

Soft moans escaped my lips as I tried to sit up. What my boss had said was a simple procedure now racked my body with pain.

How could I have been so stupid? I had always taken every precaution, but now found myself in a predicament that only an abortionist could rectify. As it turned out, the 'doctor' my boss sent me to was a butcher. My bed sheets were soaked in blood. I phoned my boss at home. This wouldn't make him happy, but not knowing if I was going to live or die nullified all fear of his anger. A gruff voice answered the phone, "Yeah?"

"I need help! Something is wrong, there's blood everywhere," I cried.

"I'll send an ambulance right over, and meet you down in emergency."

I set the phone back into its cradle, wanting to think he cared, but knowing first and foremost, I was his meal ticket.

I met him one day, working the Strip. Many of my friends I worked with were getting killed. The streets were a dangerous place to make a living, but I didn't know anything else. My so-called father taught me how to hate men, and to use my body to its full advantage. Just thinking about him caused a deep-seated anger to take over. How I hated that man! At any rate, this man introduced himself to me one night, and offered me protection for a nominal fee.

"Yeah, right." I kind of laughed to myself. But thinking about the other girls being killed, and the fear of losing my life, made my mind up for me. I became one of the many girls in his stable. For some reason, he always treated me a little better. He said I had the makings of a movie star. He made sure I worked out every day and gave me extra money for my wardrobe. It was different working for him. He set up all the calls so I didn't have to work the streets anymore.

For that much I was thankful. The night-
life on the streets always kept you on
guard, wondering if the next trick would
be your last.

But this kind of work began to take its
toll on my body and on my mind. An aching
loneliness consumed me.

Down at emergency, my boss began to
apologize, "I was sure this guy was legit."

"Don't worry," I told him. "I'll be
back on my feet in no time."

He nodded and said, "I'll be back
tomorrow to look in on you."

I was saddened. All he really cared
about was his investment, but what more
could I expect? It was the only life I
had ever known.

I was in a room with three other women.
Two of them were going to have their
babies any day, and the other woman's
baby was still born. Why I was put into
this room, I had no idea. I had killed
my baby. To me it was an inconvenience
getting in the way of my livelihood. In
my profession, I could not be strapped
down with any kid. I know I was hard and
bitter, but you had to be in my line of

work. Nobody could see inside. To keep my sanity, I had a little place in my heart where I hid away from all the horrors of life. I pretended there was actually a man who would love me for myself — not for my body, but for me.

The woman in the bed next to me was the one who had lost her baby. A man with the gentlest voice would come and see her daily. His encouraging words seemed to calm my aching soul. Even though the curtain between us was always pulled, and I didn't know what he looked like, I eagerly awaited his daily visit.

My boss never did come in and see me, but he did send some nice flowers. I guess he thought that was good enough.

I was going home. They informed me that I would never be able to carry another baby. I was relieved. At least I would never have to go through this ordeal again. The only sad thing was, I would miss the gentleman who came to visit. There was something about him that I longed to reach out and touch. But I quickly reminded myself not to get those warm fuzzy feelings. Men had a way of ending up hurting or destroying you. They were a species you couldn't trust.

My boss gave me a few more days to rest once I returned home. Then it was back to work, but something was different. I tried to fight these feelings, which were at war in my soul. It was like a hidden part of me was being exposed. I was sick of these men using my body for their own pleasure. There had to be something else I could do to make a living. I was beginning to change. I wondered if it had been what the man had said daily to the woman in the bed beside me. He had talked freely to her about a man named Jesus Christ.

The following day was Sunday, which I actually had off. Before, I had not thought about it being a Sunday. A day off was a day off. One year I'd bought a suit for an office party. I decided to wear this, as my other clothes would have given my profession away. I headed for a nearby church. I was definitely being drawn, but trying to explain it, even to myself, sounded spooky.

I guess I was early. A few people occupied the various pews. I took a seat near the back. It felt cold and I shivered. I sensed people looking at me, and began to feel like I didn't belong there. With my street—acquired boldness, I stared right back at them. They quickly turned away. Glancing around, some of the men looked familiar.

I decided I'd seen enough. These people did not want me here and I didn't want to be taking up their space either. What I had sensed in the stranger was not in here. I headed for the streets once again, disappointed that I hadn't found what I was looking for.

As I walked, different men turned their heads to stare at me. I had **that** kind of look. Sometimes I wished I were ugly, so that men would not look at me.

I found my way into the little park at the end of my street, and sat down on a park bench. I watched as families picnicked beside the pond. In my dreams, I would belong to a family. There was a loving father you could talk to and be friends with, a mother who would wipe your tears away and hug you closely, sisters to share your dreams and desires — yes, a perfect family. But the bitterness of the past would creep in and spoil my dream, filling me again with hatred and fear. I could not shake off the fears that held me bound. I was startled by a voice speaking to me. Tears had been coursing down my cheeks that I hadn't been aware of.

"Are you all right, Miss?"

His voice sounded familiar. I looked up and glanced over at him. I wanted to nod, to say yes, everything was fine, but what happened next surprised me. I began sharing with him all the anguish in my soul. Like a volcanic explosion, I spewed out my twisted life experiences. Once started, I couldn't stop. I shared in detail about my home life growing up, then about my life on the streets. I sat before him fully dressed — yet fully exposed. He then took my hand in his and bowed his head. His gentleness touched my heart. I knew deep inside that what this man was offering me was a love I had never known.

"Heavenly Father," he began, "in Your mercy and in Your love, please touch her and make her whole once again. She doesn't know what love is, how You sent Your only Son to die for her. Reveal Your love to her now. I ask this in the name of Jesus Christ."

I was sure now. This was the same voice, which visited me each day while I was in the hospital. I wanted to explain how I knew him. He wasn't in a hurry to get away, even though he'd heard all about my disgusting past. He asked me to accompany him to an evening meeting he would be involved in. I hesitated. My experience with church left me cold inside. He didn't push me, but waited for my response. Well, I figured, what did I have to lose?

Just a minute, this isn't a church, I thought. I had passed this warehouse many times on my nightly stroll. But thinking back, many of us had ridiculed the events going on in this building. We made fun of the young people giving out pamphlets, and even threatened them. Now I was entering this building. I hoped no one would recognize me.

My new friend motioned for me to sit near the front as he proceeded up to the makeshift platform. He picked up a guitar and strapped it to himself. As he began to strum the instrument, the music picked me up and began to rock and comfort me. Tears flowed freely down my face, and I didn't care at that moment who recognized me. I found myself lifting my hands, then my arms, toward heaven. An incredible love began filling me. I invited this man, Jesus Christ, to come and live in my heart. I knew I would even be able to face my earthly father, and forgive him with this forgiveness I found. This man Jesus Christ was a man I could trust.

I spent more and more time at the warehouse they called a church. Because of my new convictions, I could no longer sell my body. My boss told me I would never make it in this new 'society', that sooner or later I would come crawling back to him. My decision bothered him, but I knew what I needed to do.

The pastor presented me with a book called the Bible, and helped me understand the passages, as we read the pages together. I had once been marooned on a desert island, but now my thirst was quenched with these words, which were streams of living water to me. I realized with each word I read, my past was forgiven. I was able to start a new life.

As I began to grow in this newfound faith, I realized taking the life of my baby was wrong. I asked God to pick up all the broken pieces in my life, and to heal me so I could carry a child once again. Somewhere in the future, I would find a mate, one who would truly love me, and we could be the family I always dreamed about.

The pastor was able to locate a job for me as a receptionist. I took typing in high school, and this helped me clinch my new job. I found I really had a special gift for making people feel accepted and loved.

What the evil one had meant for destruction, God turned around for His good pleasure.

# Passage Eight

———❧———

You were once enlightened to the truth, you knew the Way. What happened that you became so hardened, and bitterness took you captive once again?

Did you look to people to fulfill your heart's desire?

What draws us to look to this present world to supply our physical needs? Are we afraid to trust in a God we can't see with our physical eye?

What does it mean to walk by faith? Is the Bible reliable? What took place nearly two thousand years ago? Is this event relevant today?

So many questions accost us at every turn. We want to believe the truth, but life, in all of its twisting, ever turning ways, keeps us tossing to and fro.

We find deception in the church. This is supposed to be a place of health and healing. Instead, we find a place full of 'self'. Everyone is sure they possess the ultimate truth, knocking down their brother or sister to get their point across. Where is this love they so freely preach?

A brother or sister falls into sin. The church's response is often to shoot the wounded soldier. Where is the love Jesus Christ displayed on the cross when He cried, "Father, forgive them, they do not know what they are doing."

Beware of false prophets, who speak blessing and then curse in the next breath. Satan's strategy is to use your brother or sister to deter you from following the truth. He roams about as a roaring lion, seeking whom he may devour.

Look at the prodigal son. Watch closely as the scene unfolds before you. Here was a son who took full advantage of his rights. He had a right to his inheritance. He took his inheritance, and spent it on his newfound friends and on himself. He quickly spent it all. Soon his friends disappeared and he found himself alone. After some time of living hand to mouth, wearing the same clothes day after day, he remembered his father's servants would have their needs looked after. So after much contemplation, and humbling himself to serve in his father's household, he started for home. Nearing home, he saw a familiar figure coming towards him, his arms outstretched, welcoming his long lost son.

So . . . for you, who have wandered away from your heavenly Father, there is a way of return. Don't let religion and unforgiveness keep you from coming back into the Father's Presence. Time is so short. The day of salvation is today. Do not harden your hearts. Let Christ come in, cleanse you, and bring you back into the Light. Jesus leaves the ninety and nine to seek out that one who is lost.

Is it you?

# Passage Nine

—∞∞∞—

I could feel myself falling, and knew when I hit bottom I would be dead. But it seemed at the last second, a hand came out of nowhere and gently set me down.

When did I lose touch with reality? How had I sunk so low that I didn't even want to live? Wouldn't death be a reprieve after what I was experiencing? Yet somehow I knew that if I died now, hell would have won.

How many years had passed? I vaguely remembered leaving home, telling Dad to go to hell. He hadn't understood how I needed those friends to stay in the 'in' group. I was tired of trying to live up to his expectations. I accused him of not loving mom enough, and of not spending time with her. That was why she left with another man. At this point I remember him slapping me soundly across my face. Screaming obscenities at him, I told him

I never wanted to see him again. "Consider me dead!" I said viciously, slamming the door in his face.

I was free at last. For a while it was great being with my new friends. But with the lifestyle I was settling into, I occasionally found myself in jail. This was a dangerous pack I was running with, but the booze and white powder I was snorting drowned all the warning signals out.

My first encounter with this fine white powder left me seeking more. I was on a magic carpet ride. I could go anywhere I wanted — do anything my heart desired. I remember one night, looking at a picture and actually floating into the picture. It was heaven!

Because my habit was expensive, I had to steal and manipulate to score cash. I found myself doing things that were degrading, even inhuman. The white powder owned my body and soul. Sometimes the powder wasn't available, so to take the edge off, I drank.

Over time, my pack of friends began to dwindle. Some committed suicide, some were put behind bars, and others were killed in freak accidents. Now that only two of us remained, she became my best friend. We really hit it off. But I wondered now, as I sat in the corner of a dark hallway, what had happened to her. A voice filtered into my consciousness. She was begging me to come with her. She said she had found help to get us off the drugs, which were killing us. I guess I wasn't ready to let go, and told her to have a nice life. She said she loved me that she wouldn't let me go. She promised she'd be back for me. I watched her walk away. Part of me wanted to go, but I felt the way back was beyond my reach.

My magic carpet rides were now rides to hell. Evil creatures constantly pushed me, faces snarling, their fangs dripping with blood. Their voices were my constant companions. They'd goad me and taunt me, telling me my days were numbered. They mocked any goodness that once had been mine. I was in total darkness. It suffocated me.

On one particular night, after scoring a few grams of my death angel, I began to float towards a bright light. It was peaceful until the light began to take on a grayish hue, then total darkness surrounded me. An evil voice filled me with terror, beyond any terror I had ever known. "Tonight you die, you are mine. You will spend eternity with me!"

What came forth form my mouth then completely startled me. "No, you can't have me! JESUS HELP ME!"

The evil one prodded me with his boney finger. "Jesus can't help you now. You sold your soul to me. Just step off this ledge, and your worries will be over. You know you can't hang on any longer — come with me."

Was I losing the battle? Where was Jesus? I began to panic. At that moment another voice penetrated the atmosphere.

"Don't do it, son. You have your whole life before you. We are here to help you, don't jump."

I looked down. Beyond the small ledge I was standing on, an expanse of empty air stretched to the street below. How did I get here? I began to inch my way to the sound of the voice.

"That's right," the voice coached, "just a few more steps and you will be safe."

That's all I ever wanted, was to be safe. Strong arms held my shaking body.

\*\*\*

This was the first time I had been introduced to a treatment centre. Even in the jails, you had access to drugs, but not in here. I was being turned inside out. My body would enter into levels of semiconscious states, and evil beings taunted me.

"Did you think you would escape us? You belong to us!"

Evil laughter covered my soul. I entered into one horror filled scene after another. I wanted to escape, but where could I go?

The voice I heard on the ledge was taking authority over the evil that smothered me. "In the name of Jesus Christ, and with the blood of the Lamb, I come against you satan? Loose my son and let him go. I bind the spirits of addiction, rebellion, and fear in the mighty name of

Jesus Christ. Take your filthy hands off my son, and let him go!

The strongholds that that held me bound were actually leaving. I could feel them tearing one last strip off my soul, and then I spewed them forth from my mouth.

Oh, what light permeated my being, and the warmth, it enabled me to feel once again. I was free at last. I opened my eyes for the first time in days. The form of a man was kneeling by my bedside. I reached over and put my hand on his head. My lips were cracked and bleeding, but I whispered, "Thank you, you saved my life."

The man looked up. I looked into the eyes of my dad. I tried sitting up, and he gathered me into his arms. We cried with one another long into the night.

\*\*\*

I sat near the back of the large auditorium, and listened to the man who was instrumental in bringing me back from the brink of death. I scanned the faces, and what I saw made me sad. They were lethargic. Some nodded in agreement, but others nodded off and were actually sleeping. Why were they even here? Didn't they know Jesus? Didn't they know about the resurrection power available to them? Didn't they know they could do exploits in the name of Jesus Christ? His name was the most powerful weapon they possessed. They were being deceived by the evil one. I gripped the hand I was holding, my best friend and soon to be my wife. She nodded, reassuring me I should say something. I rose to my feet and made my way to the aisle. Heads turned around, wondering what the commotion was all about. Ushers tried to stop me, but I headed to the front with determination.

The pastor had stopped speaking and waited as I made my way to the podium. We met in each other's arms, and held one another for a few moments. I whispered in his ear that I would like to say a few things. Tears slid down his cheeks and he stepped back, giving me his podium. I suddenly felt fearful, looking over the sea of faces, but then an inner strength began to take over.

"I was lost and now I am found. Jesus left the ninety and nine, and sought me out, and brought me back into the fold. Your pastor is my dad." I knew some of them never knew he had a son, and this sent flurries of whispers throughout the crowd. I waited for silence and continued. I began sharing the experiences of my past. "Rebellion led me into hell, my addictions kept me bound, satan wanted my soul."

I exhorted them to never give up, to pray through for souls, that the name of Jesus Christ and the blood He shed on Calvary were powerful weapons available for them today. Sitting in a pew on Sundays was not enough. They needed to take these weapons and use them in the sewers of life. There were ones like me that needed to be rescued. My dad came into the sewer of my life and tossed me a lifeline. This was love in action.

"During my release from drugs, I threw up all over my dad, yet he still held me in his arms and took authority over the evil in my life. I was a stranger to Dad and he took me in. I was naked and he clothed me. I was sick and he visited me.

I was in prison and he came to me. I was thirsty and he gave me a drink. I didn't deserve this, but Dad gave what he had — Jesus Christ. I saw Jesus Christ manifest in my dad."

Tears flowed down my cheeks, and I could hardly speak, but I still managed to say, "If you're out there today and you need to be set free, Jesus Christ is the only Way. Jesus Christ is Truth. Jesus Christ is Life. Jesus Christ desires to set you free."

The whole congregation stood to their feet and began clapping, and praising Jesus. The front of the church filled with people on their knees, crying out to God, and seeking His Son, Jesus Christ.

# Passage Ten

———⌇———

I was a passenger, though no one seemed to notice I was here. We were sailing on a small craft. A wind came up out of nowhere, and we all began to bail water as the gigantic waves threatened to turn us upside down. The men bailing water were drenched. Each wave pounded against the boat with such fury, I wondered how we would survive.

I was sure Jesus had stepped onto this boat. Where was He through all of this? Someone else must have read my thoughts, for one of the disciples cried out, "Get Jesus before we all drown!"

Another disciple ran to the stern. I followed him. To our surprise, there was Jesus, sound asleep. My first thought was, how could He sleep through such a storm?

The disciple shook Jesus. "Master," he shouted, "wake up! We are in the middle of a storm, the boat is sinking, and we are all going to drown." He spoke in hurried phrases, trying to get Jesus' full attention. Jesus wasn't in a hurry, but He did arise, and walked with purpose to the bow of the boat.

Jesus rebuked the wind, and spoke to the sea. "Peace be still."

As quickly as the wind and the sea were stirred up, they now became very calm. I looked out over the water. It was as smooth as glass. The disciples were as shocked as I was.

Jesus turned to them, "Why are you so fearful? Why do you have so little faith?"

My eyes were riveted to His. He was speaking to me as well. I couldn't breathe. I wanted to have faith. Where does one purchase this kind of faith? He heard my thoughts.

"Faith comes by hearing, and hearing by My Word. Faith is also a gift, and will be given as you require it." He spoke these words directly into my heart.

Later, I could hear the disciples speaking amongst themselves. Such a fear had taken hold of them. "Who is this man, that even the wind and the waves obey Him?"

He truly captivated my heart, this man Jesus, and it was my heart's desire to learn everything I could about Him as he spoke to me through His written Word.

# Passage Eleven

---

"Mommy, Mommy! I'll be good, please, you're hurting me!"

Was it my little boy's screams, or the strong hand gripping my arm, that brought me back to reality? Two men in blue uniforms towered over me as I looked down upon the cringing form of my little boy. The weapon in my hand was pried loose. I began to shake all over. What was going on? One man was soothing my son. He picked him up in his strong arms, and carried him towards the door.

"Where are you taking him?" I screamed.

"To the hospital," the policeman replied. "He's taken quite a beating."

Looking over to my son, I saw his shirt torn with blood seeping through gashes on his back, angry welts on the side of his face, and blood trickling from his nose. Terror filled his little eyes. As I went to approach him, he flung his arms about the neck of the policeman and began to cry. "Please don't let her hurt me anymore!"

"It's okay son, you're safe with us, and no one will hurt you again."

"Please, I didn't mean to hurt him, he's all I've got, please don't take him away from me!" I begged.

My pleas fell on deaf ears.

I looked through the open door and recognized my neighbor. "You're to blame for this! Always nosing around, lurking in the hallways, spying on us! Because of you, I'm going to lose my son!" I spit a few lines of obscenities at her.

The policeman who put the cuffs on me interrupted my tirade. "Look, lady, if it hadn't been for the concern of your neighbor, your little boy could have been killed. You better be thankful she cared enough to give us a call."

I could hear the other officer asking questions, and my neighbor answering each one emphatically. "This hasn't been the first beating, she beats him regularly. And he is such a good little boy, very polite and actually quite a happy boy. I live above them, and tonight when I heard him screaming, I couldn't stand her abusing him any longer. I just wish I had called you sooner. For that I am guilty. I know she has been through a lot, losing her husband and all, but for the life of me, I can't understand why she would take her frustrations out on her little boy."

I began to realize the seriousness of my predicament, but all that was happening didn't seem real. Maybe this was a bad dream, and I would soon awaken from it. But as the police dragged me to an awaiting car on street level, the horror of what had taken place started to sink in. I was angry and scared. What really troubled me was that I didn't seem to care anymore. They could lock me up and throw away the key. I didn't care!

My husband had taken the easy way out as far as I was concerned. If I had known the kind of financial trouble we were in, I could have worked to help out. But he didn't think it was necessary to tell me anything about his business dealings. I thought we were wealthy by the way we lived. But thinking back on it, my husband always was high-strung and lived a very fast paced life. I remembered the night, the phone call, and the trip to the morgue. Yes, that was my husband. He had shot himself in the head. The memory still brought queasiness to my stomach. After all his bills were paid, the money that was left over was enough to set up a meager apartment, and that was about it. I found a job easily enough, but I had to leave my son alone. There wasn't enough money at the end of a paycheque for babysitting. I can't remember why I started beating him. I loved him very much. I needed to be a father and a mother to him. When I was growing up, my father always beat me, so I figured it was the way to train your kids. But it was more than that, and I wondered if I would ever find out. Actually, when my husband was alive, he would look after all the discipline and never laid a hand on him. I didn't agree with this kind of discipline, but my husband was the head of the house so I didn't interfere.

They put me in a cell by myself. As I reminisced over the past year, I felt nothing towards my husband, my child, or myself. All feeling was gone. I was shutting down.

I sat in the courthouse and awaited my sentencing. The judge heard the charges against me. I could feel him staring at me but I kept my head bowed and stared at my feet.

"Please look at me," demanded the judge.

I looked up and fixed my lifeless eyes on him.

"I'm sending you to a treatment centre. They specialize in emotional trauma, which I believe you are suffering from. When you are well, you will be brought back and assessed. We will then look at the charges of abuse. For the time being, your son will be given to your parents who will look after him. They have come forward on your behalf."

As I heard this last statement, I was shocked. I hadn't seen or heard from my parents in years. Why would I contact them when my growing up years with them was a nightmare? I hated my father for all his brutality, and despised my mother for not stepping in and helping me. New waves of bitterness crashed in. My son would be in the hands of this monster. But I didn't have the strength to speak up on behalf of my son, so I kept silent. They'd soon find out for themselves, these caretakers of humanity.

I came face to face with my parents in the hallway of the courthouse. They sure had aged since I'd seen them last. Mom hugged me right away but Dad hesitated not sure how he would be received. It was strange being hugged by Mom, we had never been demonstrative at home. Looking at them now, they seemed different, but I couldn't figure out what the change was.

"Dad and I will be praying for you, honey," Mom said. "We have found new hope, and when you are ready we will share this with you. I know the treatment centre you will be going to. Our pastor visits there regularly. If you want, we can come and see you."

"Yes," Dad agreed, "there are so many things I need to ask your forgiveness for. If I could just go back in time and do things differently." Tears slipped down his cheeks, and he didn't seem to care who saw them. "I love you. We should have been there for you, especially when your husband died, but we were so caught up in ourselves back then. You don't have to worry about your son. We will take really good care of him."

Who were these people? This man was not the Dad I remembered. His philosophy with children was that they should be seen and not heard. He had never, in my whole life of growing up, sat down and had a decent conversation with me. The parents I remembered were far from peaceful, but I could sense peace in them now. What a mystery this was. A new tiredness weighed upon my shoulders. I fidgeted, wanting to get away. I was relieved to see a guard coming.

"Time to go, Miss."

Both parents hugged me, and I turned and walked away with the guard. I wanted to turn around and wave, but they were strangers and I didn't know them anymore. I was asked if I wanted to see my son. I declined. I didn't want to hurt him anymore. I had seen the terror in his eyes. I was his enemy. He'd be better off if I just stayed out of his life. Being reunited with him seemed impossible.

\*\*\*

At the treatment centre, the doctors probed and prodded my psyche as I slipped deeper into a deep dark hole. Anger, hatred, fear, and bitterness strangled me. I was being asked questions that I didn't want to come to grips with. I wanted to be left alone. Maybe my husband was right. If life lets you down, just end it all. But I didn't have the means to end my life in the treatment centre, so I would have to wait until I was let go. But my departure from this place was not in the near future. One doctor told me I was not co-operating and that I could be here for quite some time.

I looked forward to the prick of a needle, knowing then sleep would come, and I could forget all the fear that continually assaulted me.

My parents came at regular intervals, and at one time offered to bring my son. I made such a commotion I was sure they'd never bring up the subject again. Each time they left, they would offer up a prayer for me, speaking to a God I didn't know. They prayed with such a familiarity with this God, it was like they knew Him personally. I tried not to react one way or the other. That's all I needed right now, to become religious. No thanks! I didn't believe it was that simple. Accept a God you couldn't see, and then live happily ever after. It was a fairy tale as far as I could see. No, I had to live with the consequences of my own actions, and that was that.

\*\*\*

Six months had passed since I was sent to the treatment centre. One day I sat watching other patients. If I ever got to that point where I would sit and rock myself like some of the patients were doing, then for sure I needed someone to shoot me on the spot. To me that was proof of being totally crazy.

I was now able to converse somewhat with the doctors, and I could tell they were pleased with my progress. I still found it difficult to talk about my past. Anger towards my husband for leaving me to face his death and the long list of bills began to fade. I guess I accepted this, and began to feel sorry for him that he had chosen to take his life. It really was a cop out. I decided, coming to this conclusion, that I wouldn't take my own life after all.

In one of the sessions, the doctor, probing, asked me why I beat my son. What had caused such anger to surface that I would beat on a helpless child? My answer scared me. I told him it was vengeance. I was getting even for what happened to me as a child. As I sat on the chair, I pulled my legs up, hugged my knees to my chest and began to rock. The startling revelation shook me to the core. I began to cry, quietly at first, but then my body started shaking uncontrollably. The doctor came to my side and put his arm around my heaving shoulders. I was going crazy! He ordered me a sedative, and I was taken back to my room. As I lay there, my eyelids heavy with the medication, I began to wish I could be normal. I wanted to be free from the fears holding me in their grasp. I decided to see the pastor mom mentioned each time she came to see me. With this thought in mind, I drifted into a deep sleep.

The next day I requested a visit from the pastor. That afternoon he spent some time just getting to know me. He didn't seem to be religious at all. He was a very simple and humble man. From what I pictured ministers to be like, well, he didn't fit the description at all. Could I trust him? I wasn't quite sure, so some of my burning questions would have to wait. That's one thing I had on my side, time. I wasn't usually allowed outside, but because of his request, we strolled through the many gardens surrounding the centre. The fresh air and smells of the garden seemed to renew me. I looked longingly at a rose. So perfect, how each petal was formed. And the smell, I had forgotten how beautiful it smelled. I drank in the smells and sounds of the outside world. I wanted to be set free, to experience life once again. Was it being with this man that gave me this yearning, or was it something else?

Each week after that outing in the garden, a new rose appeared on my night-stand. A love gift from the man of God. I looked forward to his visits. I came to the conclusion I could trust this man. I really wanted to pursue a relationship with him. I was lonely for a man's company. All the other men I'd known only wanted a sleeping companion. I wanted more.

The pastor often spoke about a rela-tionship he had with a man named Jesus Christ. I was curious about this man Jesus, and determined not to get trapped in religion. But the more I heard about Him, he didn't seem religious either. My pastor friend explained what happened when Adam, the first man on earth, and Eve, the first woman on earth, sinned. They became separated from God. Because of this sin, God sent His only Son to die on a cross, so we could have a way back to the Father. Maybe this was why I felt so empty and lonely. I needed a way back.

During one visit, I knelt with the pastor in the garden, and put myself into the nail-pierced hands of Jesus Christ. He was real and His life engulfed me. I wept and with each tear shed, a cleansing took place inside me. I didn't speak out loud, but I gave Jesus all my anguish, anger, bitterness, rebellion, fears. I gave Him my all. My pastor friend hugged me. Maybe I could have a relationship with this man one day.

I was eager now to see my parents. I wondered if they would notice that I had changed. The doctors knew something was happening, as I didn't need medication anymore. I was on my way to recovery. It was Jesus who was giving me a new reason to live. I still struggled though with the thought of seeing my son, or even if he would want to see me. He would be twelve years old now. My parents had filled me in on his progress. He was receiving counsel to overcome his fears from the abuse I had put him through.

The day my parents arrived I noticed they were not alone as I looked through my window my son was with them. My heart started to race and the palms of my hands were sweaty. He looked so grown up I ached to hold him. I was sure my pastor friend set this up. I wasn't angry with him, I loved him for his thoughtfulness but was I ready to see the life I nearly destroyed?

A gentle knock on my door brought me back to the reality I was facing. I hesitated for a moment and breathed a prayer to my newfound friend. He was there with me, His presence covering me with His strength, so with confidence I opened the door.

I stood facing my son. He was alone. He stood for a few minutes in the hallway, he looking at me, me looking at him.

"Hi Mom," he said shyly, "I've missed you."

Shocked by his words, I gathered him into my arms and began to weep. "Oh, I've missed you too. Please forgive me for hurting you. I love you so much."

His arms hugged me fiercely, as he began to sob. "Mom, I forgave you a long time ago, Grandma and Grandpa took me to church and in Sunday school a lady told me about Jesus Christ. Mom, He's my best friend. I tell Him about all my hurts and disappointments. When you didn't want to see me, I told Him and He told me He would look after you."

I listened to this young man, and my heart poured forth thanksgiving to my heavenly Father.

"Son," I replied, "He answered your prayers because I know Him as my best friend as well."

The tears that had been held back for so long now flowed freely between us.

I didn't know how long I would be detained at the treatment centre, or what kind of sentencing I would receive on my charges of abuse. This new lease on life I had been given, and knowing my son was near, would be enough to take me through.

# Passage Twelve

—❧—

I stood at the edge of the clearing, and wondered what my next move would be. I had been suspicious about my wife's whereabouts for quite some time, and now I possessed the truth. She was having an affair.

We both decided not to have children until our careers were firmly mapped out. But in the years following our fairy-tale romance and subsequent marriage, a distance grew between us. Lately, though, when I wanted to spend more time with her, I received a cold shoulder and broken dates. I heard my own words coming through her. She told me she had a business to run, but she would try to spend some time with me soon. Anger and bitterness crept over me. Hadn't she taken the time to involve herself with this new man, and where did I fit into this scenario?

I reached into my jacket and pulled out the handgun I had recently purchased. Nobody was going to take my wife from me and get away with it. It seemed the only way to remove this intruder from our lives. I still found it hard to believe that my wife would take this stranger to our cabin hideaway. To me, the place was sacred. Our love for one another had flourished here.

I parked my truck on the main roadway, for I felt the element of surprise would give me the edge. As I approached the cabin, perspiration trickled down my forehead and my hands trembled. I had hunted many times before, but now the thought of shooting a human being was unnerving. I wouldn't kill him, just put him out of commission for a while. That was my plan.

I didn't bother knocking. I opened the door and found my wife and her lover in a locked embrace. Something inside me snapped. Desperate rage swept over me.

The intrusion caught them both by surprise. Horror filled my wife's eyes when she recognized me. I pointed the gun at the stranger and pulled the trigger.

My wife screamed, "No!" instantly putting herself between him and bullet. I watched her crumple to the floor. The stranger started coming at me, so I fired again, and he collapsed, inches away from my wife.

This whole scenario was so bizarre; I couldn't believe what was actually taking place. I moved over to where my wife lay, and took her into my arms. Blood oozed from the hole in her chest, and I could hear myself crying, saying, "No, not you, I only wanted to scare the guy. Please don't die." But as I looked into her ashen face, I knew she was dead. Hearing the stranger's groans, I realized I had to get help.

I was out of breath once I reached my truck. After I called 911, my body began to shake. Searing pain tore through my chest as the reality of what I had done hit me.

Wailing sirens and flashing lights of police cars approached me from a distance. I dreaded what would happen now.

The only person I truly loved was dead, and I was the murderer.

*****

I know my lawyer was just trying to help, but I knew I wasn't insane. I was tried and found guilty of first-degree murder. Yes, I had thought about it. But no, my wife wasn't the one I wanted dead, it was her lover. Why she took the bullet for him, I would never know. As luck would have it, he survived. I was sentenced to lethal injection. I didn't care at this point. My life was over. I had nothing and no one to live for.

******

As I sat on death row, I had eons of time to think about what I had done. I wondered what death was like. What was it like for my wife during her last moments? I shivered. I still couldn't get that image out of my head. It replayed over and over in my dreams.

It was eerie, hearing the priest talk to the person in the next cell, giving him his last rites, then walking with him down that long hallway, knowing it would be his last walk.

Months crawled by and I still didn't know when my day would come. But that was the way the system worked. I no longer had any rights, and they didn't have to confer with me on anything.

Memories entertain me. My mom had been a very religious person. She would often read me stories out of a book called the Bible. She took me faithfully to church every Sunday when I was a little boy. One day Mom became very ill, and the next thing I knew, she was lying in a casket at the front of our little church. I came to the conclusion then, that if God (if there was such a person) would let my mom die, I didn't want anything to do with Him. My mom was all I had. I never knew my dad, since he left before I was born. So I had grown up on my own, and as far as I was concerned, did quite well by myself.

The business world was a cutthroat society, where one had to step on many a

person to reach the top of the ladder.
In fact, you had to keep looking out for
number one. I worked long hours to estab-
lish my own company with people working
for me, but now as I sat here in this
cell, it seemed all in vain. I signed
over my company to an associate, the only
person I could trust.

My friend told me he was in the process
of appealing the decision handed down
by the judge. He said he would hire a
top-notch criminal lawyer. This being my
first offense, he felt someone with more
expertise could have me out in no time.
I tried to talk him out of it, but my
friend was determined to help.

After six months of waiting, and gru-
eling loneliness, a letter came to the
prison. It was a stay of execution from
the governor. I was re-sentenced to fifteen
years. Being moved from death row, I felt
sad. I guess I had been psyching myself
up for death, and it seemed disappointing
that I would not be granted this way out.
Living was the harder road to take. I
wanted to stay by myself and not mingle
with anyone else, which on death row was

easy, as no one was allowed your cell. But in this end of the prison, a new set of rules required you to be constantly on your toes. No one was friendly. Sullen looks, sneers, and cursing were all that confronted you, moment to moment.

Always sitting behind a desk in the working world, I did physical exercise daily. I was glad this had been one of my priorities. Men stayed away from me because of my muscular strength.

Hate is a breeder of hate. The evil, which surrounded me, engulfed me. Inside my loneliness, I found a spot where I could spend some restful hours, and no one could touch me.

One day, a man met me there in one of my quiet moments. I was shocked and wondered how he came to be there. He didn't speak but just looked at me, sadness in his eyes. I didn't know what to say. I felt peaceful with him there, but wasn't quite sure how to handle the situation.

It was late one night, after the last guard shone a light into my cell, I felt myself drifting off to sleep. A bright light suddenly lit up my cell, jolting me upright in bed. The outline of a man could be seen in the light. My heart began to race. My eyes, now adjusting to the light, saw that the man sitting in the chair across from me was the same man I had seen in my thoughts. Had anyone else seen him come in? The light was so bright I was sure it would wake up the other men in the cells around me, yet the light seemed to permeate my cell only. I felt peaceful in this light. My heart slowed down, and I wasn't trembling quite so badly as before. I finally managed to speak. "Who are you?"

"I am Jesus of Nazareth."

Shock and disbelief penetrated me. I tried to think back to the stories my mom told me about this man. Were these more than stories? Here was a man sitting in my cell claiming to be Jesus of Nazareth. I rubbed my eyes again and knew I wasn't dreaming. He was still sitting there, looking right through me, it seemed.

What he said next, branded me for life. "I have come to set you free. This world cannot set you free. Freedom comes from a relationship with Me. Death doesn't free you as you might think. There is an eternal being in each human. There is a heaven and a hell, and you must choose where you want to spend eternity."

This man sure had a way with words. My eyes gushed with tears that had been locked up in my soul for so long. I cried over the death of my mom, I cried over the loss of my wife, and I cried because I was a murderer and only deserved death and hell. The man moved from the chair to the side of the bed. He held me in His arms, a Father I never knew holding me, comforting me, showing me how to let my emotions loose. I held Him close, too. He felt human, not some ghostly apparition. I began to stammer like a little kid. "I-I-want-want-you-to-come into my heart, Jesus. Please cleanse me and make me whole."

Fresh tears flowed from my swollen eyes. I felt clean inside. I knew I was a brand new person. He gave me a whole new lease on life. It didn't matter where I was. I knew now that when I left this earth, I would live eternally with Him.

The next morning, the glow in my cell lingered. I knew then it was not a dream. I couldn't see Him but I knew He was living in my heart, the center of my being, and He would never leave me.

I asked one of the guards if he could find a bible for me. He looked at me strangely, "I'll see what I can do."

A couple of days later, he showed up with a tiny pocket book. "This was all I could find. Looks like only the New Testament to me."

"Thanks, this is great!"

As I began to read, the words seemed to leap right off the pages and fill my heart with excitement. I had a burning desire to share this new treasure I had found. This happiness could be an answer to all the pain and hopelessness confronting me daily.

In one afternoon, I had read the entire book. In the next reading, I pondered over each word, letting it settle into the deep recesses of my heart. They were such powerful words; I knew that I could climb mountains with the information I was receiving. I wondered how I could share these words with the men around me. In the business world, I remembered I could talk circles around my competitors. I sensed these words could change the prison world and the business community around. I would not have to lie or cheat. I would begin today.

I started reading my little book out loud, first the gospels and then the rest of the New Testament. Some of the men didn't want religion pushed down their throats and made crude remarks. Because my reading was causing agitation, the guards threatened to take my book away. In fear that one day they would do that very thing, I began to memorize the words. No one could take it away from me if it was in my heart.

This project took me a year to complete. I shared about Jesus whenever I had the chance. They called me the 'preacher man'. It felt good to be called that. I didn't consider myself a murderer anymore. When Jesus came into my heart, He wiped my slate clean. I would explain this to some of the men that met me daily for bible reading and prayer. Several men gave their lives to Jesus Christ. Sadly, though, they thought this meant Jesus would miraculously set them free from prison. When this didn't materialize, many let go of their faith, and went back into the dark holes of unbelief. I tried to explain that if you wronged society, then you would have to pay. Laws were set in place for our protection. People had to be protected from those who broke the law.

The principle of sowing and reaping worked in confinement, as well as in the free world. If you sowed evil you would reap evil.

Jesus Christ gave us His life so we could be free to love and to give hope to the hopeless. I guess if I hadn't had Jesus Christ living inside of me, what I was sharing would be hard to believe. But having Jesus living in my heart, it made perfect sense.

I was seeing through different eyes. Men hated me because I tried to be the model prisoner, but I didn't hate anyone. I wasn't rude to any living soul. I wanted

Christ's love to shine through me, and I tried to help anyone in need.

\*\*\*\*\*\*\*\*

After serving eight years, the Parole Board deemed me reformed. I would be a free man in two weeks. I wanted to say that I was a free man all this time, but wasn't given the opportunity. It doesn't matter where you are, because freedom comes from within.

When I returned to my cell that evening, I knelt by my bed and returned thanks to my heavenly Father for allowing me the privilege to serve Him. I thanked Him for granting me physical freedom. I looked forward to spending the rest of my days witnessing of His miraculous Presence within.

# Passage Thirteen

———❦———

Anticipation filled the Synagogue as Jesus entered. A man with a withered hand was in our midst.

It seemed to me that the Pharisees were always on the lookout, trying to accuse Jesus of something. Why weren't they as thrilled as we were? Someone had come onto the scene of sorrow, sickness, death, hunger, loneliness, depression, and all other evils that plagued mankind, to set the people free! Jesus only did good. I really wondered, what was their problem? Could it be jealousy? Everyone was drawn to Jesus. After all, Jesus had a solution for every problem He was confronted with. I still couldn't help but be completely over-whelmed with the miracles Jesus performed.

A hush penetrated the room when Jesus spoke to the man with the withered hand. "Step forward."

Jesus looked around the room and asked, "Should you do good or do evil on the Sabbath, kill or save life?"

The Pharisees knew He was asking the question of them. They kept silent but fumed within themselves.

I could see anger in Jesus' eyes as He spoke to them, yet He seemed grieved at the same time. "Your hearts are so hardened," declared Jesus.

Jesus turned to the man with the withered hand and said, "Stretch forth your hand."

The man, in obedience, stretched forth his hand, and it became as whole as his other hand. The man cried out with joy as he lifted his new hand and waved it in the air, rejoicing.

Praises from all over the Synagogue filled the air. I found myself praising and crying out to God. What a miracle! Such joy burst forth as we all stood, giving praise and thanksgiving to God.

News spread quickly about the man in the Synagogue, and soon throngs of people were following Jesus. It grew more difficult to get close to Him, but I pressed on through the crowds.

I had to stay close to Jesus. He was the answer to all of my questions.

## *Passage Fourteen*

———— ∞ ————

I wrapped the flimsy, nearly threadbare blanket, around my shaking shoulders in the chilling night air. I huddled as close to the inside corner of the large cardboard box as I could. A gust of wind came up from out of nowhere. This was going to be a frigid night.

\*\*\*\*

My mother and father died in a fatal automobile accident just after I turned five years old. As there was no known family, I was handed over to the Child Welfare Services. After some months, a distant Aunt and Uncle came forward, saying they would look after me. These strangers moved me into their small apartment, and quickly spent my parents' estate.

Grief for my parents subsided as new grief erupted. My so-called aunt and uncle began to physically and mentally abuse me. Nearly every night, I silently screamed for someone to rescue me from this horrible nightmare. Why were these people so set on destroying me? Why had the system given me over to these monsters? I knew I would have to run away, but I didn't know where I could go.

Five years crept by. When I turned ten, new dangers assailed me. Being left alone with my uncle one night turned disastrous. I remember vividly, his face looming over top of me. He roared, in his drunken state, that he would teach me a few things about life. Men deserved respect and could take what was due them. I did not understand at first, but as I grew older, I realized he took my virginity. How I hated that man! Why did I have to keep on living?

As I sat reflecting over my past, the future looked just as bleak. Several of the homeless girls sold their bodies for extra money. They encouraged me to join their ranks. Recalling the anguish I felt when my uncle fondled me, I vowed no man would ever touch me like that again. I'd rather starve, and there were days when I nearly got my wish.

I remembered turning thirteen. My aunt and uncle were now staying in a beat-up motel, as they were constantly on the move. I woke up one morning and the room was deserted. I almost cried for joy! But what now? Where would I go? I had been living mostly on my own anyway, but I'd always had a roof over my head. Now I would have to provide that for myself as well. Still, I was so relieved my aunt and uncle were gone, I cried for hours. After pulling myself together, knowing someone from the motel office would soon be at my door, I bundled my clothes into a pillowcase and wandered out into the street.

****

Night after night, I slept in alleys, on park benches, in bus stations, and wherever I could find a place to lay my weary head. I quickly learned street sense, and dressed like a boy so men would stay away from me. I worked at odd jobs, and with my meager pay, managed to eat once in a while.

I had been living on the street for three years now. I was bone tired, and on this particular night, finding an empty box under the freeway seemed to be a godsend. Just as I was falling off to sleep, I felt someone jostle the box. A stranger held me fast. Fear shook me to the core. "Look," I gasped. "I'm sorry, it didn't look like anyone was here. It was getting dark and I didn't want to be left standing on the street. If you'll just let me go, I'll be on my way."

The stranger's hold on my arm relaxed, but still did not release me. I was now standing outside, looking into the weather-beaten face of an older woman. We eyed one another closely and a smile appeared on the woman's face.

"Sorry for scaring you like that. I wasn't sure if anyone was in here or not. You're just a youngster, where are your parents?"

I was just about to answer but she kept on talking.

"This is no place for children. Just the other day, a friend of mine was minding her own business and was stabbed in broad daylight. This world is an evil, evil place. So answer me child, what are doing out here?" She motioned me back into the box with her.

I hesitated, not knowing what to do.

"Look, I'm not going to hurt you, and you can't stay out on the street. We'll figure something out in the morning, but for now you'd better stay here with me."

I nodded and went back into the box with her. It was a little crowded but I was thankful for her company. Her presence brought hope for the first time since being left by my aunt and uncle.

"I don't have any parents. And I'm not a child. I'm a woman, almost sixteen." I thought I better clarify myself. For some reason, I didn't want this person to think I was a boy.

"So, you're an orphan then?"

I nodded. But realizing she couldn't see in the darkness of the box, I managed to say, "yes." My teeth were chattering and I didn't know if it was the cold or nervousness, being with this stranger.

She seemed to understand. She sat up and put her arm around my shoulder. "Don't worry about anything. Annie will look after you. The good Lord always looks after me. I'm sure He sent me here so I can repay His kindness and help look after you."

I didn't know anything about a good Lord, but my fears began to settle down as I let my head rest against her. Sleep came quickly.

****

Annie looked down at this sleeping form and lifted her face heavenward. "Heavenly Father, You sent this wee one to me, and I will see that this soul is well taken care of. Thank you for sending me out here tonight, and showing me this waif of the street. You provide all of my needs and I'm thankful for Your constant care."

Annie glanced around the box, and hoped the real owners would not show up. She found ministering to those in need, these homeless people of her community, to be her station in life. Annie would have to gain this girl's trust, and then move her into her own home. Annie's husband had long since gone on to glory, but the money he left behind had at once been put to good use. Their large ranch house now housed fifteen children she had found roaming the city streets. Annie had never been able to have children of her own, but she was abundantly blessed with all these homeless children. Trusting her heavenly Father to supply strength for this task, Annie ministered to many disturbed and violent children. Annie was a firm believer that with lots of love and hugs, any human being could change.

Tears clouded Annie's eyes as she looked down at this face nestled on her arm. "What horror stories do you have to tell, my sweet one?"

Annie could see fear draped over the child, and knew she would need extra wisdom from her heavenly Father to help this one. Annie could not sleep. She would keep guard over her new charge, and then by morning, she prayed, this new child would trust her enough to come with her.

I awoke with a bit of a fright, realizing I was next to this stranger. As I looked up, her eyes smiled back at me. In the morning light, she didn't look like a street person. She seemed well dressed and I wondered what she was doing here in this place.

"Good morning. I'm sorry I deceived you last night. As you can see, I'm not a street person. I'm actually a missionary. I work for a man named Jesus Christ. He sent me here last night to see if you would like to come home with me."

This information totally baffled me. Why would anyone care about me? My aunt and uncle told me all along I was no good, that they did me a favor by taking me in. They never allowed me to attend school, so I couldn't read or write. Without this knowledge, I knew I could never do anything with my life. Now here was a total stranger opening her home to me. What was the catch? Everything on the street had a catch. What did she want from me? I was tired of living on scraps, moving from one garbage bin to another. Could I trust her? What did I have to lose?

"So, what do you say? Will you come and live with my family and me? If you don't like it, you can leave anytime, no strings attached."

It sounded like a fair deal to me. I nodded shyly.

We both crawled out of the box and stood to our feet. I suddenly swayed, and the woman put her arm around me to steady me. I hadn't realized how hungry I was. With the sudden movement, dizziness swept over me. The woman led me over to a pickup truck, unlocked the door, and helped me inside. I suddenly felt pan-icky. What was I thinking? I didn't know this woman, and here I was sitting in her truck. She must have seen the terror on my face, for she quickly and softly spoke reassuring words.

"Child, please trust me. If I wanted to hurt you, I could have done it in the night. Believe me, I just want to help you. This is what I do for a living, I minister to those in need."

"I don't need no charity," I said defensively, "I've looked after myself for three years. I don't need anyone!" I reached for the door handle but couldn't force my hand to respond.

Annie's eyes closed as she gripped the steering wheel. "Please, Father, show me what to do. Don't let her leave," she spoke quietly.

I sat there staring at her, wondering what she was doing. Calmness settled over me, and I took my hand off the handle. I found myself saying, "Well, maybe I could use a hand for a few days. But I'll work for my room. I don't take handouts."

We had driven about half an hour when the woman turned down a gravel road off the main highway. Towering trees lined the road, and rolling hills stretched out as far as the eye could see. My heart leapt within me. How often had I dreamed of one day living in the country? To skip through a meadow laden with wild flowers, to listen to gurgling brooks, and be free as the birds soaring in the bright blue sky. This was my greatest desire. I found myself hoping this was real. Or was I just dreaming? We then turned down a lane with a white-railed fence stretching along both sides of the lane. At the end, we came to a stop, and a gigantic house came into view. Several children bounded out of the house, running towards the truck. Their faces shone and laughter rang from their voices. I sat fixed to the seat and watched as the children leapt into this woman's outstretched arms.

"Annie, you're home! Did you find what you were looking for?" Their faces turned towards me as Annie headed for my side of the truck.

"Now children," warned Annie, "don't scare her. Let's get her safely into the house."

The children obeyed quickly. Annie took me by the hand, and led me to the large, sprawling house. Once inside, the wonderful smells of breakfast filled my nostrils. My stomach rumbled, and I thought for an instant I would be sick. Annie proceeded to take me to the kitchen, where a huge table seemed to fill the whole room. Annie seated me beside her and I watched eagerly as mounds of food were heaped onto my plate. I grabbed a fork and began gorging myself. I didn't notice as everyone else bowed their heads.

Annie began to pray, "Heavenly Father, thank you for providing nourishment for this family. Thank you for bringing us this new child. Give us Your wisdom and Your love, in Jesus' name we pray. Amen."

Fork in hand, I paused for barely a second, then continued eating. How long had it been since my last meal? I couldn't remember.

Annie didn't scold me for not stopping to say grace, but she did caution me to not eat so fast. She said no one would take my food, and I could have as much as I wanted. Tears sprang to my eyes. Someone was always stealing my food on the streets. It didn't matter where I hid it someone always found my stash.

Annie seemed to understand. "Don't worry, we will see that you are well fed. Take your time and enjoy. You get settled first, and next week we'll give you your chores."

I nodded in agreement. What a wonderful place this was! Could I really trust these people? They seemed so happy and content. Would I ever be so happy?

After breakfast, Annie showed me to my room, which I would share with two other girls. I didn't care; I finally had a bed of my own. A memory from the past made me shudder. Aunt and Uncle always made me sleep between them. So I wouldn't run away, I guessed. This way Uncle could have his way with me whenever he felt the need. It happened on a regular basis. Hatred for him festered deep within. A fear of men and hatred for them seemed to consume me. I tried to shake loose from these feelings, but I knew I was held captive.

A new dress was laid out on the bed. How did Annie know I had never owned a dress? I picked up the soft material and held it closely to myself. I had always dressed like a boy. Now I was holding the most beautiful piece of clothing I had ever seen. Before putting it on, Annie showed me to the bathroom where a huge tub filled with hot soapy water greeted me. Annie left and I ripped off my soiled clothing. I slipped down into the depths of the water and began sobbing. Oh to be clean once again. If only I could feel this clean on the inside.

Once I was dressed in my new clothes, I looked at myself in a mirror. Staring back was a girl I didn't know. Gone were the dark smudges, the tangled hair, and too-large clothes that hid who I was. It was still hard to smile, but I tried, and my mouth obeyed. I caught Annie standing behind me and I whirled around.

"Annie, why are you doing this for me?"

Tears welled up in Annie's eyes and slipped down her cheeks. She wasn't afraid to cry in front of me. "Oh child. Jesus said we are to look after the little children, and what would Jesus do if He were here? He would take you to Himself and take all your cares away. He's given me a love for children, to help them in any way I can. I love you."

"But, Annie, you don't know me. You don't know the things I've been through, the bad things I've done, and how I've survived day after day. I don't really feel like a woman. I'm sixteen but I never got to be a child."

Annie approached me cautiously and opened her arms. I hesitated, and then moved into them. It felt so good to be held by another human being who genuinely showed love.

\*\*\*\*\*\*

Several months passed by, and I was beginning to settle into this new home. When Annie found out I couldn't read or write, she immediately began to teach me. All the other children went to school, but Annie said I could stay with her for the time being. My studies were coming along quite nicely, and it thrilled my heart to be able to read and to write my name.

Annie took us to a little country church on Sundays. This was a new experience, and I didn't quite understand the love these people had for me.

One night a terrifying dream woke me and I screamed out for Annie. She was quickly at my side and held me until the fear subsided. My aunt and uncle had come for me in this dream, and the horrors of being with them made me scream out. Once again peace settled over me, after Annie took her petition before the Lord. I wondered who this Lord was. Could anyone have a relationship with Him, like the one Annie had? In the morning I would be sure to ask Annie. This God was given precedence in the church services, and it seemed everyone there was eager to give Him their full attention.

Annie went back to her room and knelt beside her bed.

"Heavenly Father, is this the time to ask the child about her past? I sense that until her past is dealt with, she can never move safely into the future. I know You can take her safely on. Please give me Your wisdom and knowledge in dealing with this young girl. She seems so fragile and I don't want to scare her. Father, I think she is beginning to trust me, and I thank you for answering me. I long to adopt her as my own, and I ask You so show me how this can be accomplished. Thank you for giving her Your peace. I love You, Lord."

In the morning, I awoke with a sense of purpose filling my heart. I just knew something special was going to happen today.

Annie seemed pleased I had found a love for horses and the rest of the animals on the ranch. So my chores consisted of helping to muck out the stalls and feed the animals.

One of the ranch hands had been kind enough to teach me to ride and today he was taking me riding on the rolling hills surrounding the ranch. When riding, I felt free for the first time in my life. I loved the wind blowing through my long brown hair and the sun shining on my face.

I quickly donned my jeans and pulled on my new boots Annie had bought me. My new clothes seemed to accent my figure, and I was beginning to trust my emotions as a woman. New beauty enveloped me, and I began to feel good about myself. Still, the looming thought of being tainted kept me from pursuing any man's attention. That area of my life was still hidden.

The ranch hand had my horse saddled, and he looked eager to get started on our outing. His eyes looked me over from head to toe and I quickly felt uneasy. Why was he looking at me like this? My face felt hot and shame covered me instantly. Memories of my uncle paraded themselves in front of me.

As he began to help me, his hand brushed against mine and I yanked my hand back, startling my horse. He reared throwing me off balance and I tumbled to the ground. The ranch hand came towards me and I panicked. I began screaming.

Annie, hearing my screams, rushed out of the house and down to the corral. She helped me to my feet. I began to shake.

"Are you hurt?" asked Annie, deeply concerned.

"No, I don't think so, just scared."

The ranch hand looked as puzzled as Annie. Annie turned to him, "What happened?"

"Look, Annie, one minute I'm helping her to take hold of the reins before she stepped into the stirrup, and the next thing I know, she's screaming and lying on the ground."

I knew then, I had acted like a complete fool, but I just wanted to get away from this man. What I didn't understand was, why was I scared of him after he had been so kind to teach me how to ride?

I felt so out of control, so I brushed myself off and ran crying to the house. I hurried to my room and threw myself down on my bed. What was wrong with me?

Annie knocked gently on the door, and let herself in. She must have known the time had come, and questions needed to be asked. Annie breathed a quiet prayer and sat on the edge of my bed.

I sat up and threw my arms around her. She was the only security I had ever known. I could trust her. I began to spill the sewage of my life. As each horrid detail came pouring out, Annie held me tightly. Silence blanketed the room as I recalled the last detail.

Annie spoke softly, "You must forgive your uncle."

I shook my head. "No, I can't do that. He ruined my life. I hate him."

"I understand that, but you are hurting yourself by not letting go of the past. The only way you can be free from this man is to forgive him."

Annie let this sink into my heart. I did want to be free, but forgiving this brute was a difficult thing to do. I had carried hatred for this man and woman for so long, it was hard to let go of it. Annie explained that Jesus Christ, once I let Him into my heart, would give me the strength to do the impossible. I wanted to know this God Annie always prayed to.

"Annie, please pray for me. I want to accept Jesus Christ into my heart."

Annie led me in a simple prayer that I repeated after her. "Jesus, I know You are the Son of God. I believe God sent You to die in my place. I'm sorry for my sin, and I ask You to forgive me. Please come into my heart."

Weight seemed to lift from me. I actually felt light filling my being. I didn't want any of my past haunting me any longer.

"I forgive you, Uncle, for hurting me and making me feel dirty inside."

Emotional dams burst, and tears streamed down my face. I forgave my aunt for not helping me, and for forcing me to stay in the filth of their lives.

At that moment, I was a new creation. My past was over and I now had a future. I prayed for my aunt and uncle that somehow they would come to know Jesus Christ too.

\*\*\*\*\*\*

The ranch hand is now my dearest friend, and we often ride the hills together. I no longer fear men. Annie's dream of adopting me became a reality. I now stand beside her as her daughter. We continue to minister, helping many lost souls come into the kingdom of God.

# Passage Fifteen

⤖

I cried myself to sleep that night. I just couldn't get used to that narrow cot they called a bed. I was used to the queen-size bed my husband and I shared for so many years. I found myself smiling. I used to complain when his snoring would awaken me during the night. I would jab him in the ribs and he would roll over, making sputtering noises. Those memories were my only solace during these lonely nights.

I was in unfamiliar surroundings, frightened and alone.

It seemed like only yesterday that my son and daughter-in-law brought me to this place, but I knew I had been here almost a year. I begged my son to let me live at home. It was the only home I had known. I loved to walk through my garden, and smell all the blossoms in the springtime. I could have my friends over

for tea, and we could chat all afternoon.
I was my own person in my own home.

The decision was made because I had
one little fall, and they said my memory
wasn't as good any more. I could remember
anything I needed to remember. My eye-
sight was getting a little dim, but I was
nearly eighty. This old body was shutting
down, but I was mentally aware of all
that went on around me.

What did they call this place? A nursing
home, or something like that. I didn't
need a nurse. I could look after myself.
I looked after my own home, my son, and
my husband. Now in my later years, they
wanted someone to look after me.

I thought back to the time when my
husband got so sick. He died quickly. I
was thankful he didn't have to suffer like
some of our friends did. I looked after
all the funeral arrangements, because our
son was traveling and couldn't come home
in time. I looked after all my husband's
business accounts and put monies away for
a rainy day.

I was proud of the fact that we helped
our son buy his first home after he was

married. Couldn't he see I didn't need anyone to look after me? I really could look after myself.

My son's wife couldn't wait until I was put away. We never did get along, but she seemed so smug about my son's decision. So, I remember telling my son I would hold him to his promise of never leaving me to fend for myself. I told them both I would move right in with them. Their children were so excited that Grandma was coming to live with them. The horrified look on the girl's face was worth it all. That conversation made me chuckle, and I felt a little guilty for feeling the way I did, but that snot of a girl deserved it. She rattled on and on about how it would never work. She fumed and fussed like an overheated locomotive. I let her squirm for quite a while before I released my hold on the situation. I finally gave in to my son, and told him he could do what was best for all involved. I wish now, though, I had held on a little longer. Life sure had its twists and turns.

I tried to get comfortable in that bed but just as my old bones began to relax, a nurse bolted into the room.

"Rise and shine! Isn't it a beautiful day?" she exclaimed as she whipped open the curtains.

The sunlight shocked these old eyes, so squinting, I put my hand over my eyes to protect them.

This nurse, I actually liked. She had spunk and didn't put up with my moods. There was something about her; she just **oozed** with that something. She was always cheerful and encouraging. I liked the way she had a hug for this old body of mine.

She opened the closet and began sorting through my wardrobe.

"Here's a nice dress that will be just perfect for today," she said, holding it up for my approval. I nodded my head in agreement. I couldn't imagine what she was up to.

Slowly, I sat up and put my legs over the edge of the bed. Did I sleep last night? I felt a little groggy. My nurse seemed to notice this and sat down beside me.

"You had a rough night?"

I wanted to answer her, but was tongue-tied. There was so much simmering inside wanting to come out, but I wasn't sure how to begin. I wasn't one to share my life with anyone. Even my son didn't know my deepest hurts or secrets.

"It's okay. You don't have to answer. I'm taking you for a walk today. It's quite a long walk, so I'll put you into a chair with wheels, and you can sit and enjoy. How does that sound? Right after your breakfast we'll head out into the bright blue yonder!"

I wasn't sure how that sounded. It would be wonderful to escape the sounds and smells of this place, of that I was sure. I couldn't understand why my son couldn't take an interest in me like this nurse did. Couldn't he remember all the wonderful things I had done for him? Wasn't this payback time? One thing about being my age was, I sure had time to think. My life had been so busy, I don't remember ever taking time off. Never would I have taken an offer to ride in a chair with wheels. I let the nurse help me dress. She was the only one, mind you that I let do this for me. After all, I could look after myself.

After breakfast, the nurse was true to her word, something my son could learn. He had promised, since putting me in here, that he would visit me every Sunday. It was almost a month since I had seen him and his family. Bitterness gripped me. I was sure it was the daughter-in-law keeping him away from me. I missed seeing my grandchildren as well. I overheard her saying once that I was nothing but a crusty old dinosaur, and didn't have anything good to say about anyone. Right now I guess that was true. But the nurse was creating a special day for me, so I tried to lift my spirits. Thinking about my negligent family would not help.

"Here now, just let me put this shawl around your shoulders, and we will be off," the nurse whispered in my ear. At least my hearing was still good.

The moment we reached the outdoors, my soul seemed to be released. It was springtime once again. My eyes drank in the spectacular blossoms, bright green leaves, and the blue-sky overhead. I took a deep breath and the sweet smells intoxicated me. Something about spring made me feel young and alive once again. Tears glistened in my eyes. Where did the time go?

"I just love this time of the year," I heard the nurse saying, "My heart nearly bursts in thanksgiving to my Lord Jesus Christ. Some of us, you know, are like winter. We lie there with no life in us, cold and frozen, and then spring comes bounding into our lives. The warm sunshine of Christ's love opens our hardened hearts, and saturates every part of our being, making us whole once again. Have you ever had this experience?" The nurse stopped, parking me in front of her, looking at me intently.

"Can't say as I have," I replied. "I'm too old for such nonsense. Never had any reason to rely on religion. Always looked after myself. My husband was that way though. He talked on his deathbed about some kind of vision; whatever that is, of putting his hand into the hand of a person called Jesus. I didn't know what to think of that. We never went to church much, just at Christmas and Easter. So I guess, dearie, I can't honestly say I've had the experience you're talking about. My husband was always kind of a softy anyway." I smiled at the remembrance of him.

"Well," the nurse went on to say (she didn't give up easy, did she?), "it's never to late to come to the cross. It doesn't matter to Him how old you are. Did you know He gave His very life for you because He loves you so much? He died so you could live." The nurse took my hand and looked deep into my eyes. The love I saw there caused tears to well up. I tried to pull my hand away, but she held on.

"Why would you care about a crusty old dinosaur like me?" I felt strange speaking the phrase my daughter-in-law used against me.

The nurse didn't bat an eye. "Because, whether you believe me or not, I love you. Just as I will live eternally with Jesus Christ, I want you to have the same invitation He gave me. Jesus said, 'Come to Me, all you who labor and are heavy laden, and I will give you rest.'

(Matt. 11:28) The Word also says, 'For God so loved the world, that He gave His only begotten Son, that whoever believes in Him should not perish but have everlasting life.'" (John 3:16)

I began to shake my head. "I don't want to live forever. This old body of mine just wouldn't last."

The nurse smiled, then laughed out loud. "You won't have the same body, you'll be transformed. Jesus will give you a glorified body, just like the one He lives in today."

All those fancy words had me somewhat confused and I guess my face showed it.

The nurse patted my hand and said she'd be praying for me. Some of her warmth spilled into my heart. Maybe there was something to this, after all. We had a lovely morning together, seeing all that spring had to offer. It was difficult to return to the nursing home, but now I had memories of this day I could draw on for months, if need be.

Instead of wheeling me to my room, the nurse walked toward the dining room. I tried to protest. But as we neared the entrance, many faces began to look familiar. Someone on a piano was playing and people were singing, "Happy Birthday to you." What a surprise! I had totally forgotten it was my eightieth birthday. I looked around, expecting to see my son, but was confronted with my daughter-in-law. My two grandchildren came running toward me, throwing their little arms around me. Oh, it felt so good. Tears were now streaming down my face. I had missed seeing them so much. Even the thought of facing my daughter-in-law wasn't so bad. She came over and kissed the side of my cheek.

"Happy Birthday, Mom."

"Thank you." I was truly thankful. Some of the words my nurse had spoken found a way to sink into a tiny crack in my heart.

Many of my old friends, from long distances away, had come especially to help celebrate my birthday. My daughter-in-law apologized for my son's absence. He was away on business, but would come and see as soon as he returned. She mentioned he had something important to discuss. After opening all my presents, and visiting with my friends and family, weariness took its toll. I tried to stay responsive, but my eyes kept closing on me. Many could see my plight and decided to call it a day. There were hugs and kisses from everyone, and my nurse finally wheeled me to my room. She helped me into my bed and pulled the covers to my chin.

"I'll see you tomorrow." She leaned down and kissed my cheek. "Remember, I'll be praying for you."

I nodded and closed my eyes.

The next morning someone drawing the drapes awakened me, but all was quiet. Something was wrong. Where was my nurse? My eyes, adjusting to the morning light, fixed on the stranger in my room. She scurried about, not giving me the time of day.

I finally managed to ask, "Where is my nurse?" She turned and looked at me, tears pooling in her eyes.

"I'm so sorry to be the one to tell you this, but on her way home yesterday, she was in a terrible car accident and died."

I mustn't be hearing right. No, this couldn't be, she was too young to die. I was the one who was supposed to die first. My heart literally began to ache. I turned on my side and sobs shook my body. The new nurse came over and put her hand on my shaking shoulder.

"There, there now. She did leave you something at the desk. Just a minute, and I'll go get it for you."

I couldn't imagine what it could be.

The nurse returned with a beautiful package wrapped in paper covered with colorful birds, flowers, and trees in full bloom. The paper reminded me of our morning together. I held the package to me for quite some time as the memories of that morning soared through my heart. The nurse left me alone with my package and my thoughts.

I carefully began to open it, not wanting to tear the beautiful wrap. Inside was a box. I took the lid off, and the words Holy Bible stared back at me. I picked up the book and it felt soft in my hands. How did she know I loved the feel of leather? Tears slipped down my cheeks and I opened the cover to find my name written inside the cover. Her next words pierced my heart. "I pray you will soon come to know the Author of this book. He is my life, and one day soon, He will come for me, and I will be forever with Him. I will be in a brand new body, not the body I lived with on earth." She had written, "Ha! Ha!" in brackets. "Please know I love you. I never met my own mother as she died when I was born. I adopt you as my mother. See you soon …." It was signed with love from my nurse.

I closed my eyes and held the book tightly to myself. I was determined to read it cover to cover. I had to find out if there was such a thing as eternal life, new bodies, and all the other things she spoke about on that beautiful spring morning.

I got up on my own, dressed, and was sitting by the window reading when the nurse arrived to take me to breakfast. She looked surprised and smiled when she saw me with my book.

After breakfast, I retreated to my room, eager to learn more about this Holy Book. Each time I picked up the book, something special happened in my soul. I didn't even notice when my son sauntered into my room.

"I've never seen you so intent on reading before, Mom. Where did you get that book?"

I looked up and smiled. Usually his visit was a welcomed sight, but not today. I just wanted to be left alone so I could read. I felt time was short and I wanted to finish the book.

"Mom, I'm sorry I missed your birthday yesterday, but I was in Houston. My company needed me there for an important meeting. Speaking of which, I want you to sign over your shares to me so we can go ahead with a new deal I'm putting together with a company overseas. I have to have total controlling shares or this new company won't deal with me. What do you say?"

I looked blankly at him. He came all this way to tell me to sign on the dotted line. He took away my home, my dignity as a human being, and now he wanted to take away the only thing I had left from my husband; the signing rights to our family company. Where did he get off? What kind of a greedy boy did I raise? We tried to give him everything, and now he wanted more. I just couldn't understand this. I wanted to stay calm but I started to seethe with anger. I put my book down and stood to my feet. I wasn't going to take this sitting down.

"Son, what do you want from me? I've given you everything. But one thing I will not part with is the signing rights to my company. You got that? You seem to forget whose company it is. You didn't have to work night and day, but I did, along with your father."

It was then he took the bait and we went head to head.

"What do you mean, I don't work? I never see my wife or kids anymore. I practically live out of a suitcase. I can't believe you would say such a thing. I didn't take your home, we never sold it, remember? Selling it now wouldn't be a bad idea, with real estate booming."

"I'm not selling my home!"

"Fine. But please be reasonable about the company. Even if you sign over your shares, you know you'll always have more than enough money. You're comfortable, aren't you?"

I looked at him with disbelief. How could I be comfortable in this place? Was he serious? The only comfortable place I knew was my home. It was then a plan began to form in my mind.

"Look, son, I'll sign those papers if you will take me back home. That's the deal. When I'm sitting in my own living room again, you can bring the papers by and I'll sign them." I felt so sure of myself, why hadn't I thought of this a year ago?

He plunked himself down on my bed and his shoulders sagged. At that moment he looked like my little boy again. I longed to hug him to myself, but I pictured this as giving in, so I stood my ground.

"Mom, I'm sorry I can't do that."

"What do you mean, you can't do that? I'll pack my things and we'll be out of here in no time. I want to go back home." I was determined to get my way this time. I had a right to be happy too.

It seemed like a long time before he spoke. "Mom, I really had hoped you would never find out. I mean, you seemed so happy in here, and I got such a good deal on the house, it was the best decision for both of us. Mom, I sold the house last month. I put all your things in storage and we can go through them later. Besides, I talked this over with your doctor, and he said you could never live on your own again. You need special care."

Everything I held dear to me was snatched away. I no longer had any control. I was past feeling anger. Bitterness balled up tighter in my heart. The feelings I had towards my son were disgust and hatred. How could he do this to me? Just when I thought I had a way out, the door slammed in my face. I found my way to a chair and sat down heavily. I couldn't speak. I wanted to be left alone. Why didn't he leave?

My son could see I was distraught. He came over and tried to hug me. I pushed him away. He then tried to kiss my cheek but I turned my head. "Mom, just think about signing those papers." He then looked at his watch. "I've a meeting in an hour, I'll see you tomorrow."

I sat for the longest time, after my son left, trying to understand everything he said. Let's see, I no longer have a home. I no longer have a say in the company my husband and I built from the sweat of our lives. I no longer have a son who used to give me time and attention. What was left for me to give?

At that moment, a voice said, "You can give me your heart."

I looked around the room, who was here? I didn't notice anyone come in. The voice continued, "This is the day of your salvation, do not harden your heart towards Me. The Words you have been reading are spirit and life. They are capable of setting you free."

I bowed my head and closed my eyes. Yes, I wanted to be free. I was tired of being angry and bitter. I really didn't understand what I was doing, but I wanted to belong to the Light who filled my nurse with such love and joy.

"God, please fill me with this Light. I give my heart to You. Please forgive me for the anger and bitterness I have toward my son. I accept Your Son Jesus Christ."

I then tried to remember if there was anything else I should be asking. I sat quietly for a few minutes, and radiant warmth covered me. It felt like I was snuggled in a warm blanket. I took a deep breath and new vibrancy filled my body. I felt like I was capable of doing somersaults with this old body of mine. At that moment I jumped to my feet. I raised my arms to heaven and thanked my new Lord and Savior for my new life. I found my Bible and eagerly started reading the New Testament. Joy and love filled my soul.

As the days moved into weeks, my hunger for the written Word increased. I listened carefully for instructions from my Master. I found the nursing home to be my mission field. Each day, the Lord would take me from room to room to share my new found faith, and give a hand to those in need. One night, the Lord woke me from a deep sleep and told me to get up and go to room 204. I found the lady there deeply distressed.

"I've been ringing for a nurse," she complained, "but no one came."

By the hectic sounds coming from the hallways, I knew every able soul was busy. I explained this to the lady, but she wasn't comforted. I sensed in her the same anger I used to have, but now wasn't the time to share. I took her hand and prayed quietly. After helping her, I stayed until she had fallen back to sleep. Back in my room, I prayed. "Thank you, Father, for showing me how to help those in distress. I'm available for You to live Your life through me. I love You."

Several weeks later my son showed up again. In his absence, I phoned our lawyer and received all the information I needed for this meeting. After looking over all the facts, I came to the conclusion that a merger with this overseas company was a mistake. I was sure that because of my son's busy life, he hadn't taken the time to clearly understand all the implications of the merger. I knew the Lord was giving me His wisdom. So armed, I waited for my son to make the first move.

"Hi, Mom. I hear from the nurses you've been quite busy. I don't want you to overdo it."

I listened in amazement as my son talked on. "The doctor tells me you are off all of your medication. Is that true?"

I nodded, but still didn't feel it was the time to speak.

"What has happened to you?"

Now here was the key to the open door. I waited a few minutes to think about what I was going to say, and told him he better have a chair. After he sat down, I eased him into my life-changing story. When I finished, he just sat there staring at me.

"Well Mom, that's quite a story. I don't know what to think. One thing I do know, you look ten years younger."

I flashed a smile at him.

"Mom, because you're doing so well, I'd like you to come and live in our home."

I was stunned. I wasn't expecting this at all. I thought he was here to talk to me about the company. Now he was offering me something I would have jumped at a few months ago, but now knew I couldn't accept.

"Son, thank you for your offer, but this is my mission field. I believe the Lord wants me to stay where I am. I've always lived such a selfish life, but now because of Him, I can be a help to those in need. I'm sorry Son, but I'm needed here. But if there is ever a time when you and your wife want to vacation together, I'd be happy to look after the children."

My son shook his head. He looked up at me with tears in his eyes. "Mom, I don't know what to say. You are a different person. I've been so busy with the company; I haven't had time for my family or my own mother. I'm sorry. I do need a vacation, and I'm taking my whole family away for two weeks this summer. The two of us have talked this over and we would like you to join us. Please think about it. We really want you to come."

I went over to my child and he stood to his feet. We put our arms around each other. As I held him, I quietly petitioned my heavenly Father to bring salvation to him and his family.

My son drew back and wiped his eyes. "Mom, I want you to know I really thought about merging with this new company, but everything began to fall apart. We no longer have a deal and I'm glad. I don't know what I was thinking to have you sign over your shares to me. I'm sorry."

Wasn't that just like the Lord to go ahead and make all the crooked places straight? I smiled to myself.

"Son, I would love to vacation with you and your family. It will be a nice time to get re-acquainted." With that said, we hugged one another again. "Good-bye Son, I'll see you soon."

I walked down the hall with him, speaking to many people as I went. I waited at the door and watched him leave. I felt I wouldn't be seeing him again on this earth, but brushed aside the thought. I was eager to see my heavenly homeland, but there was still so much work to be done here. I looked around at all the hopelessness and vacant eyes staring back at me.

Three nights later, I heard the Lord call my name. It was time to go home. I left a letter to my son, leaving my Bible in his care. I asked him to give the book a chance to explain itself, for I knew he would find the words to be life changing. I said good-bye to my daughter-in-law, telling her I loved her, and asking her for forgiveness for all the years of grief I caused her. I left articles of material possessions for my grandchildren, but most important, I left them each a Bible with their names written in the front.

# Passage Sixteen

---

I was being whisked away once again, transported into another era.

I stood with throngs of people on a dusty road, back in Biblical times. Intense smells filled my nostrils, and my eyes eagerly scanned my new surroundings. It seemed everyone was waiting in expectation. Eyes lit up all around me as a man approached. It was Jesus of Nazareth. Being near this man Jesus, my heart readily burned within me. Nothing else was important. Merely being near Him and listening to His voice caused a deep yearning in my heart, a yearning to follow Him. To do and be what He wanted me to be was my desire.

A man's pleading voice brought my attention back to the scene unfolding before me. "Please, Jesus, my only daughter is dying, and I know if You touched her, she would be made well once again."

Jesus didn't answer, but I could tell it was His intention to help this man's daughter. He started following the man to his home. But each step was awkward, as the multitudes pressed in on Him.

Out of the corner of my eye, I saw a woman determined to draw closer to Jesus. I could hear her speaking. "If I could only touch the hem of His garment, I know I will be healed."

In her condition, the Law would ban her from people, as she would be deemed unclean. Her determination was paying off as she pressed in closer to Jesus. I could see her straining, reaching out her arms toward Him. Just then she made contact. I could see it in her face, in her eyes, she knew she was healed! Tears clouded my eyes. I was overcome with thankfulness and praise for this man, Jesus Christ.

Jesus stopped. "Who touched me?"

Peter, the closest disciple to Jesus at that moment, spoke up. "Master, how can you ask such a question? We are being thronged with people, and You are asking who touched You?"

"Yes," Jesus said, "I perceive power going out from me. Somebody has touched me."

I looked over to the woman. She was still caught up in her healing experience, but now fear showed in her eyes. Knowing she must come forward with what took place, she excused herself and stood trembling in front of Jesus. She then knelt down and explained vividly to all in hearing about her physical ailment. She went on to explain that when she touched the hem of Jesus' garment, she felt the flow of blood cease, and knew that she was healed.

Jesus smiled and lifted her to her feet. "Daughter, your faith has made you well. Be of good cheer and go in peace."

Grateful tears ran down the woman's cheeks and joy permeated her. I watched her until she disappeared into the crowd surrounding Jesus.

I thought about all the people I knew who were plagued with disease and ailments physicians couldn't heal. Jesus was and is Healer. Faith is a key to receiving health for physical bodies. What further surprised me was that Jesus didn't ask the woman if she knew Him, but He applauded her for simply believing. Why then, in this present day, were there so many conditions and why the simplicity of healing so difficult to find? As I weighed these questions, another man approached Jesus and the man with the dying daughter.

"Don't trouble the Teacher any longer. Your daughter has died."

Jesus glanced quickly to the man, "Do not be afraid, only believe. Your daughter will be made well."

This last statement Jesus spoke bewildered me. If the daughter was already dead, how could she be made well? Maybe he was talking about her being with His Father, and that she would soon be in heaven. I sensed this was what the father of the daughter was thinking. At least he would not be afraid, for he heard heaven was a beautiful place.

We were soon outside the man's home. The wailing and moaning sent shivers up my spine. Grief began to have its sway over everyone.

Entering the house, Jesus took Peter, James, John, and the father, and forbid anyone else to come in. I followed in behind them and stood near the door. Jesus turned and looked at me, but didn't ask me to leave. My heart began to do flip flops, and my stomach churned. I could feel something supernatural was going to happen, and Jesus was allowing me to watch.

Mourners were stationed in the house, wailing and moaning over the little girl. Jesus spoke, "Do not weep for her. She is not dead, but only sleeping."

The mourners began to ridicule Jesus because they could see with their own eyes that she was dead. Jesus then asked all the mourners to leave except the child's mother.

Jesus walked over to the girl and took her by the hand. "Little girl, I say to you, arise!"

Shocked, the spirit of the little girl returned, and she immediately sat up. I nearly fainted. Death was at the command of this man. But Jesus was no ordinary man. He walked in another realm. I distinctly noticed through all of this, He didn't want any fanfare. To Him, this was a normal thing to do, to help those in need. I thought back to the healings I had witnessed. So much emphasis was put on the healing. Our eyes were to be on the Healer. As we walk in Him, He would heal those ones who needed a touch.

I heard Jesus telling the parents not to tell anyone about what had happened. But everyone would know. The little girl was dead and now she was alive. Jesus didn't want any attention.

Multitudes now followed Him. I knew I would follow Him. I wondered though, would I follow Him merely for the miracles, or would I follow Him because deep love was burning in my soul? I decided the latter was my motivation. I truly loved Jesus Christ.

Do you?

# Passage Seventeen

———— ∞∞ ————

I stepped closer to the edge of the cliff, and looked down to the waves crashing against the rocks. My heart pounded in my chest. Just one more step, and I could forget about all my troubles. I didn't know what else I could do. I just couldn't take another day of the turmoil I found myself in. Oh, god, I was depressed.

I stepped back and sank to the ground, hugging my knees to my chest, and stared out over the horizon. How did everything get so complicated?

I twisted the cap from the bottle and let the fiery liquid run down my throat. Even this didn't dull the pain clutching at my heart. My eyes felt blurry from lack of sleep and my stomach rumbled. I had no idea when I had last eaten. For a while, alcohol had kept my head above water, giving me the confidence and reassurance

I lacked. But now, this confidence builder was ruining my life.

It would be easier for all concerned if I ended it. My wife would get the insurance settlement, and I wouldn't have to see the hurt coming through the eyes of my daughter anymore. Tears flooded my eyes, thinking about my family. Over the years I had always looked after them. But the fast pace of a wheeler-dealer took priority. I wined and dined all the corporate leaders, and found myself abandoning my family more and more. As time few by, alcohol completely took me over. I no longer could control my drinking habits. Disgusted with myself, I stayed away from home, not knowing how to cope. So my wife kicked me out, not allowing me to see my daughter. I guess I deserved the treatment, but now I just wanted a glimpse of the happiness I once thought was mine. I drove by our house, hoping to steal a glance of my family. There they were, sitting at the picnic table, laughing and looking adoringly at a man I didn't know. My chest tightened. I wanted to kill him. But the realization stunned me. My drinking and carousing caused the disaster I was facing. Now I understood why my wife wanted a divorce. If only I could go back and start all over again.

Wasn't it just today, or was it yesterday, my boss called me in and fired me. He said he tried to get me help but I was too proud to accept it. I didn't need him or anyone else. If only I could fight this demon of alcohol then I would be okay. The voices were constantly ridiculing me.

"You don't need this life, just jump. Life let you down. Go ahead, something better is beyond this realm."

There were many stories about the hereafter. I didn't believe them for a minute. Once you died, you died, that was it. That's why this way out sounded so reassuring. I didn't think I would be missed. I'd be a weight off everyone's mind. I tipped the bottle, but now all the fluid was gone. I didn't even remember drinking it. Darkness covered me as I sat on the ledge of the cliff. I don't know how long I had been sitting there, but now the desire for another drink filled my senses. I groped around looking for the extra bottle I'd brought along, but couldn't find it. I needed more confidence to jump, so thought I should head back into town for another bottle. I was down to my last few dollars, but where I was going, there was no need to worry about spending money.

I laughed. I didn't remember the last time I had laughed. One of the reasons I married my wife was because of her infectious laughter. She could get total strangers to laugh with her. Her bright smile attracted people. But in the last few years, I never even saw her smile. Her eyes didn't light up for me anymore. But a few hours ago, I saw her laughter had returned, and she seemed to glow for this new man in her life. Thinking about this, I knew the plan to take my life would be worth it all. I wouldn't have to bear any more hurt or disappointment. My wife used to accuse me of hurting her, and after my rampages — oh, the hurt and disgust that tormented me.

I'd heard once that suicide was a selfish act. But now I was sure it was the cure-all. I wasn't being selfish. I was looking out for my family.

I did try to quit drinking once, but some little thing would always lead me back to the spout. I would tip my head back, open my mouth, and let the comforting liquid soothe my soul. Yet now, I no longer felt comforted.

I made my way back to my car and started it. I looked over at the passenger's seat, and there in clear sight was my extra bottle. I sighed with relief. I really didn't like to drink and drive. I was always afraid of killing someone else. I turned off the car. I placed the bottle to my lips and took a small sip. I couldn't keep my eyes open any longer, so I recapped the bottle, and let my head fall back on the seat.

*******

I was suffocating. My lungs were blocked. I was headlong into thin air. Then there was silence. Was I dead? Evil beings were gripping my body. Yes, I still had a body, and with all the strength I had within me, I tried running away. My heart raced. Sweat poured down my face, and terror spurred me on. It was so dark. Evil laughter darted in, out, and around me. If this was death, where was the peace? Where was the peaceful state I was looking for? So, taking your life isn't what it's cracked up to be. There is no real death. I was horrified at this thought. How then, could one escape?

*********

Tears poured down my cheeks. I gripped the phone so tightly my knuckles were white. Just hours ago I felt nothing could hurt me anymore, but as I read a letter from my husband new anguish assailed me. He wrote he was going to end the hurt and frustrations of life by killing himself.

I prayed fervently. Please be there, please pick up the phone. I had just been with this man who answered so many of my questions. He now knew the hell I lived through each day of my life since I had removed my husband from my daughter's life and my own. I didn't know how to help him, this husband of mine. Booze and other women were more important to him than his own family. I couldn't bear another day with this man. But now I knew of an answer for both of us. Would it be too late?

"Hello."

The sound of his voice comforted me once again.

"Pastor?"

"Yes, I'm here. What's wrong?"

"I just received a letter from my husband. I think he's going to kill himself!"

"Don't worry, I'll be right over."

I breathed a sigh of relief, but anxious thoughts engulfed me once again. I looked up to my newfound friend and whispered His name, "Jesus, You know where my husband is and what he is experiencing, please help him, please be with him and show him Yourself."

\*\*\*\*\*\*\*

I was being hurled through a dark tunnel. Evil voices screamed obscenities at me. I had never experienced darkness as

I was experiencing it now. Hell was real. This realization caused hopelessness. I wanted a second chance. Remembering all, the second chances my wife gave me, I guess I deserved hell, but for all eternity? My heart ached for one last glimpse of my wife and daughter. I wanted to ask for their forgiveness, for all the pain I put them through over the years. I couldn't remember if I asked them in the letter. I didn't want to hurt them any longer, and I hoped the letter would explain this.

*******

The doorbell rang. I hurried to the door and collapsed into the arms of my pastor and his wife. They held me securely for quite some time, and then led me over to the couch.

"When did you receive the letter?" my pastor asked.

I paused, saying, "My husband — he must have been here this afternoon. The envelope was in between the front door and the screen door. I found it when our daughter went out this evening with a friend."

I handed the letter to him and waited as he read it through.

*****

Heaviness settled over me. I'd seen so many desperate people in my line of work. If people only knew that suicide was not the answer. Jesus Christ is the only Way, the only Truth, and the only Life. A desperate man wrote this letter, and he meant business. The act could be taking place at this precise moment. So taking my wife's hand and the hand of my newest convert, I closed my eyes.

"Heavenly Father, You are love. We know this from Your written Word. We do not know where this husband is, but You know all things. Reveal Yourself to him now. Show him there is a way out through You."

I let go of the hands I was holding and stood to my feet. A mighty boldness came over me. "Satan, in the name of Jesus Christ, I bind you and your cohorts. Take your hands off this husband, in Jesus' name. Let him go!"

\* \* \* \* \* \*

It happened so suddenly. One minute evil laughter and darkness swallowed me, but now I was enveloped in light. This light was blindingly white, and peace settled over me. I could see an outline of a man through this light.

\* \* \* \* \* \* \* \* \*

As my boyfriend drove, I snuggled in closer beside him. Being with him made me feel safe. I knew going up to the Point was wrong, but I needed to be loved. We had protection and besides, we loved each other. I was excited and scared of the consequences, but I wasn't going to feel guilty. I wasn't going to be the one to back down now. As we approached the Point, my heart sank. Another car was already in our spot.

"It'll be okay, we'll drive a little further on," my boyfriend said. But then I recognized the car.

"Wait a minute! That's my dad's car." Our vehicle barely came to a stop before I leapt out, and ran over to where Dad had parked. I looked in. No one was there. I could see empty bottles scattered inside, but Dad was not there. By this time, my boyfriend was at my side. It was nearly dawn. The sun, just beginning to peek over the horizon, helped us to follow the path to the cliff's edge. Fear paralyzed me. I couldn't look over the edge. My boyfriend spotted the form of man sprawled on the rocks below. He scrambled down the embankment. Reaching the body, he yelled up at me.

"He's alive! Call 911 on my car phone. I'll stay here with your dad."

I stumbled backwards and then ran to the car. I called 911, and sank against the side of the car door, sobs shaking my body. "Oh, Daddy, please be all right. I need you."

\*\*\*\*\*\*\*\*

"I know who you are," I heard myself say. But how I knew this, I wasn't quite sure. I don't remember ever going to church, although I mimicked and sneered at churchgoers. I hadn't needed a crutch. Jesus Christ was for desperate people. I always felt condemned when these church people came around me. But standing here with this man, I didn't sense any condemnation. I really wanted to be with Him. Suddenly I was sorry for all things I had done to other people, and especially to Him. I was sorry I hadn't lived for Him while I was living on earth.

Jesus Christ discerned my heart and said, "Because of the prayers of My children, I extend to you an opportunity to invite Me into your heart."

I immediately nodded, "Yes. Please come into my heart. I desire to live eternally with You. Forgive me for hurting You and not living for You. I believe You are the Son of God."

He drew close to me and put His arm around my shoulder. "You are forgiven."

*****

I felt a hand in each one of my hands, and slowly opened my eyes. Staring back at me, were my wife and daughter. Tears coursed down their cheeks as they gripped my hands. I somehow knew I wouldn't be with them much longer, so I motioned for my wife to come closer.

"Please forgive me. I truly love you. I'm sorry for all the pain and heartache I've put you through. A few moments ago, I gave my heart to Jesus Christ. He's asked me to live eternally with Him."

My wife bent over and kissed my bearded face. "I know," she said, "that is what we prayed, my pastor and I."

I then looked over at my precious daughter. She looked at me through red puffy eyes, and I somehow prayed she would see the new light in my eyes.

"Daughter, don't ever give up on life. Forgive me for not being there for you, for not being the Dad I should have been. Give Jesus Christ a chance. He can make all the difference in the world. I want to see you again — over there," I said, as I looked towards heaven. Jesus was standing not too far off, and I was eager to leave with Him. I continued to hold her hand and whispered, "Goodbye, I love you."

I then squeezed my wife's hand, and took the hand of my Lord and Savior, Jesus Christ.

# Passage Eighteen

C rucify him! Crucify him! The words, dripping with anger and cruelty, came forth from frothing mouths, twisted with hatred for a man they didn't even know. Didn't they know He healed blind men? Didn't they know He made the lame walk again? He brought to life a young man who was dead, and a young girl as well. He healed all sickness and disease. No evil could be found in this Man, for He was good. What had He done to deserve such a cruel death? Had these people gone mad? Wasn't it just two days ago, Jesus rode into Jerusalem on a donkey, and the crowds were hailing Him as King? Now this angry mob was crying out for His death. How could this be? Tears clouded my vision as I searched frantically for His disciples. Where were they? Was there no one to help?

I finally spotted Peter warming his hands by a fire. Surely he wouldn't let them take the Master. But somehow he looked different. A young girl came to his side and asked if he was a follower of Jesus. I couldn't believe my ears when he denied knowing Jesus! The girl insisted he was a follower, and told this to the guards around the fire pit. Peter lost his temper and swore, saying he didn't know the man. I watched as Peter quickly turned his back and fled into the night. This didn't make sense. Peter loved Jesus. He was always with Jesus. What caused him to act this way?

I glanced back at the horrific scene. Stripes were being laid upon Jesus' back and blood splattered everywhere. I felt any second now I was going to faint. The gruesome spectacle had my stomach churning and my head felt light.

"Oh, God," I cried, "Why is this happening?"

A voice surged into my soul. "That My Word is fulfilled. I must die so that you can live. I AM the sacrificial lamb, My blood being spilled out so you can have a way back to My Father. Do not fret, only believe, and you will live eternally with Me."

These words were meant to calm me, but I sobbed, "No, You can't die!" I tried shouting above the din. "Please, you're killing an innocent man."

No one listened to me.

This nightmare had to end. But as the hours passed by, darkness draped itself around my soul.

Jesus was forced to carry a large wooden cross through the square and up a hill called Golgotha. Some of Jesus' followers watched in total despair. I felt abandoned and so afraid. At the end of this road, the Roman guards actually nailed Jesus to that cross. Bile filled my mouth and I crouched down by some bushes, my stomach heaving and heaving. There was no rationale in what was happening. I looked up and Jesus was speaking.

"Father, forgive them, they do not know what they are doing."

I remember Jesus talking several times about forgiveness. Was this, then, true forgiveness? Jesus forgiving men, these cruel men who nailed Him to the cross. Why had they done this?

A voice spoke to me once again. "Sin nailed Me to the cross. Your sin nailed Me to the cross. But I took sin out of the way, so you could come to Me. This is not the end, I will rise again."

These words did not make sense to me. How could I nail Him to the cross? I was just a witness. Such darkness shrouded the hillside, and the ground began to shake and tremble. I searched desperately for something to hold on to. I shut my eyes and groped around. I flung my arms around a post and hung on for dear life. People screamed all around me. The wind whipped, lightning flashed, and torrents of rain fell, drenching me. I don't know how long I hugged the post but soon an eerie calm filled my soul. I felt something warm run down the side of my face. At first I thought it was my tears, but to my horror, it was blood. I was gripping the cross of Christ. His blood was covering me, I wanted to flee, but couldn't. I knew deep within that I needed His blood to cover me and set me free.

Soon, two men took Jesus' body off the cross. I followed them to where they laid Him in a tomb. They wrapped Jesus in white linen and laid a cloth over his face.

Some of the soldiers were ordered to seal the tomb with a huge boulder, and then to guard it the rest of the night. I stayed close by; sensing something glorious was about to take place.

Early the next morning, Mary was the first to arrive at the tomb. The boulder was no longer sealing the entrance of the tomb. I looked in with her, and to our surprise, the body of Jesus was no longer in the tomb. What Jesus spoke to me was true. He did rise from the dead! Death could not hold Him.

Mary was frightened, thinking someone had taken Jesus' body during the night. There was a man standing near by. Mary, thinking it was the gardener, asked him if he had seen anything. The man spoke Mary's name and Mary's eyes were opened. Jesus spoke softly to Mary and told her to tell the disciples that He had risen. He told her that He would come to them shortly.

I looked into His eyes, the eyes of love, knowing for all eternity I would be with Him. I thanked Him and great joy filled my heart. He wanted me to share with everyone, Jesus is alive and He is able to set us free.

I knew from that point on, Jesus' Words are true. Everything happened just as He said it would. We can count on His life-changing Words.

# Afterword

———

Someone — Somebody — was calling my name! In all this swirling darkness I strained to see, to hear. Who was calling me? I tried to answer but the words seemed to get caught in my throat. Anyway, who would want to come into this mess I called my life? No one cared about me. I was lost. No one cared whether I lived or died.

There it was again! No longer a whisper. Someone was calling me!

This time I managed to ask, "Who are you?" Even before I asked this I knew who He was. Fear took hold of me once again. He couldn't see me like this. I was a mess. I had to clean up before I could invite Him inside.

That was definitely a knock. . . . .

I was desperate. What would He think of me? I had never let anyone inside this place before. I was a pal with all the evils of the world. Now I was sick of all the loneliness, the persistent fears that held me bound, the bitterness, the hatred, and the murderous thoughts in my soul.

I wanted out!

With all the strength I could muster, I opened the door . . .

Facing me was the most beautiful Person I had ever seen. His eyes shone and emanated such love, a love I had never known. I forgot all about myself, and feasted on His Presence.

Stepping into His outstretched arms, we became one, He in me, and I in Him.

I asked Him repeatedly to forgive me and I told Him how sorry I was.

"Forgiven," He said. "I will not remember your past any longer. You are a new person. The old person has passed away. You are a new creation."

I was given a second chance. I looked around at my new surroundings. There wasn't any darkness, not even shadows. I was in total light. The scales fell from my eyes and I could see. Incredible lightness filled me. He said He was calling me upwards to my new home in the heavens that He had prepared for me. While I was here on this earth, I was to be an extension of Him, doing those things that were pleasing in His sight. He also explained that times would come when I would be tempted to go back into my old life. I was distressed at the suggestion. Why would I go back to that sewage? He assured me that when temptation came, I would have the power to resist it in His name. I assured Him I would never be tempted to go back. Sadness came into His eyes as He looked at me. I truly didn't want to hurt Him. I loved Him, and I loved my new life.

I began my journey with this man called Jesus Christ. I thirsted and longed to be with Him always. He gave me His written Word, and I read it faithfully everyday. His Words filled me with awe, and I could sense new strength coming into every fiber of my being. Bread for my soul. A light to my pathway.

I noticed other people on this journey. I had not seen them before, I was so consumed with my new friend, Jesus, and being introduced to His Father. Spending time in their Presence, I really hadn't noticed anyone else. Some of them really seemed to know much more than I did. Wanting to be like them, I followed close behind. I went to all their meetings and explored all their sayings. What they were saying sounded just like what my Father would say. It was the way they began to say that what they had found was the only answer. All other establishments were wrong. They were lifting themselves up.

What had Jesus said to me in our meeting times? He said He would be lifted up and draw all men to Himself. Then how could what they were saying be true? I called on the name of Jesus, and He met me the moment I called.

"What happened to these people?" I asked Jesus.

"Why did you take your eyes off of Me?" He responded.

It pained me to think I had let my Lord down. I asked Him to forgive me, and peace filled me once more.

I found it was a daily struggle to keep my head above all the evil that assaulted me. Why was this Way so difficult to walk in? It started with merely a thought. I began to think how easy I had it in my other life. Sometimes it was easier not to walk by faith. I mean, walking by faith took so much work! It was a work to believe. It was a work to read a book I hardly understood. It was a work to get up in the middle of the night and pray for someone I didn't even know. When was I going to have some pleasure? After all, didn't I deserve it?

I looked around one day, and didn't know where I was. I didn't sense any peace, and a foreboding fear had gripped me once again. Where was the Light? Why didn't I sense the Father's Presence? Evil laughter taunted me, and I felt so alone. The evil presence said Jesus had left me and I was on my own once again. I was dirty and didn't deserve to be any where near the Light. I was lost and . .

I remembered faintly, Jesus telling me if I was tempted by evil, I had power in His name to resist evil.

"I resist you, devil, in the name of Jesus Christ. You can't have me back, I belong to Jesus Christ!"

Suddenly a glorious Light permeated me. I was home! "Father," I cried, "how did I get so caught up with evil?"

My Heavenly Father scooped me up into His arms and said with such love, "I have bought you with a price. You no longer live, as far as this world is concerned, you have died, and your new life is hidden in Me. You are not your own. You must allow Me to be your Lord, as well as your Father and your Friend. You see, without Me, you can do nothing. Greater am I who is within you than he that is in the world. Your mind must be renewed with My Words. I will never leave you and I will never forsake you. But I will never go against your will. You are not a puppet, you are My child. As you spend time in My Presence, and get to know My Ways, you will not be so easily distracted. I have given you a Teacher and a Trainer. The Holy Spirit is His name. He will guide you into all truth. This journey is a process, and you can take only one step at a time.

"So rest with Me this day, My little one, for I will take you to where I am, and We will be one for all eternity."

# Destination

Is there safety in the midst of the storm? Is there healing for the sin-sick souls?

Is there peace for the war-torn lands?

Jesus Christ is the answer.

Jesus Christ stands at the door of your heart and knocks. He is a gentleman. He only comes in when He is invited.

God Almighty speaks to the restless heart, the empty heart, the stressed heart, the lonely heart, the aching heart, the broken heart, and the sin-infested heart.

"Come to Me all you who labor and are heavy laden, and I will give you rest." (Matt. 11:28)

Jesus Christ is your freedom from the evils of this present world system. There is no other way; for Jesus Christ is the Way, the Truth, and the Life.

Jesus Christ laid down His life for you so you could live eternally with Him. This is true love manifest in the flesh. His love reaches down through eternities past, takes hold of your heart, and changes you into a new creation. The old selfishness passes away and a new self emerges. This is the miracle of a new birth. No other religion can manifest this miracle even though many have tried to copy it. This new birth lives in the realities of Christ in you, your hope of glory. The new creation life is wrought in Christ.

You wonder if He can be trusted? So many voices are calling, "Come, this is the way, follow us!" My friend, there is only one way, and the Way is Jesus Christ. God is not a man that He would lie to you. His Word has stood the test of time. His Word does not fail. You can trust Jesus Christ to take you safely through to the other side. His Word proclaims, "I am the Way, the Truth, and the Life. No one comes to the Father except through Me. I am the Door. If anyone enters by Me, he will be saved, and will go in and out and find safety." Many are looking for a way out of the circumstances they find themselves in. Jesus Christ is the Way.

Your final destination doesn't have to be death. You can have eternal life. Go ahead. Take that step. It will lead you into the arms of Jesus Christ. It is a step worth it's weight in gold. You can walk those streets paved with gold in heavenly places.

Reach out and take hold of the hand of Jesus Christ. He is the Light. He waits with arms wide open and outstretched to you. Let your darkness be exposed to His Light.

# *My Journey*

I was traveling on a dusty road,
Though weary, I found no rest.
My soul was withered and almost dead,
Yet I searched on in my quest.

Passing many others on this road
I saw their smiles had faded too —
At first, we laughed and joked a lot
In that broad gate we walked through.

But soon the laughter died away
On this one way course we chose;
I looked back to find the way I'd come
But the gates had now been closed.

So desperately, I searched and ran,
Trying to find some place to hide
From the evil laughter mocking me —
And all this emptiness inside.

I cried out to God in my despair,
His reply came suddenly —
A Man with eyes so full of love
Stood right in front of me.

I ran into His outstretched arms
And He held me, oh so tight.
He cleansed me, filled me with His love;
I walked from darkness into Light.

It was Jesus who had saved me
And made my life brand new —
Now I'm walking on that narrow road
With Heaven in full view.

Please, let Jesus be your refuge,
Come and walk with us today.
He'll accept and love you as you are
If you just reach out and pray.

By Gwen Tymo (nee Eastland) 1955-1986
Barbara Engels' sister

CPSIA information can be obtained at www.ICGtesting.com
Printed in the USA
LVOW07s0312180414

382169LV00001B/11/P